Nephilim Wars

Book 3

By Abbot David Michael, ThD

Glentivar Village Press
POB 301, Hartsel, CO. 80449
ISBN # 978-0615845616

Edition 1.2
Fully Copyright Protected
April 2013

Prologue

The idea of wars of humans against the Nephilim as the final battle for truth is staggering. These wars have occurred all through history where the seed of Adam has warred against the seed of Sama-el also known as the serpent in the Garden of Eden who was the father of Cain. These wars continue on today with the Illuminati claiming to have the highest percentage of Nephilim blood. Because of this, the Rothschilds and their relatives consider themselves to be gods and the rest of human kind a lesser species that exists only for their good pleasure.

In addition to the Illuminati, those of Merovingian ancestry also claim to have a high percentage of Nephilim bloodline traced back to Charlemagne who was considered to be more Nephilim than human.

In this book, I will attempt to provide sufficient information to prepare the human resistance who will rise up to combat the rule of the unholy Roman Empire. This Papal-Temporal Merovingian alliance will have armies deployed around the world that will be led by Nephilim generals. Their mission will be to identify and destroy all human resistance – especially those of the male bloodline of King David. In the end, there will only be one bloodline that remains to rule the earth and the universe.

Index

Index – Cont.

Saint Michael Fighting Sama-el also known as Satan

Saint Michael will fight with us in the Nephilim Wars with over 120,000 super-powerful angelic troupes. We are not alone in this battle and should not fear since YHWH is with us. YHWH will send Y'Shua and his armies in the final hour of battle to strike the final blow against Satan, against the false prophet, the antichrist and the beast. He will bring down the Nephilim regime of the NWO and all of its followers.

Chapter 1: Safe Places During the Coming Collapse
Avoiding Disaster Hot Zones

Hot 'no live' zones include places where there is a high probability of disaster due to its geographic proximity to disaster origin centers. Places to avoid would include areas where one is up-wind of nuclear facilities (missile or reactor sites), known earthquake faults, coastlines where tsunamis are likely, natural resources that would be highly valuable to foreign governments and places or pathways that are likely for a foreign invasion.

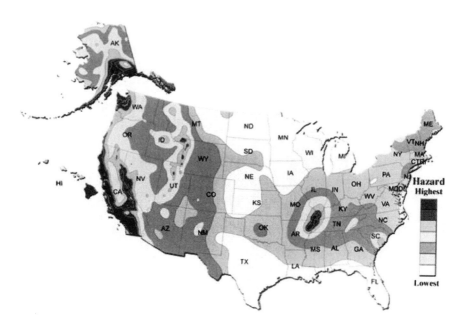

Earthquake Zones

The map above shows the areas where there is a high probability of earthquakes in the US. The dark areas on this map are to be avoided. The lighter areas are safer. Better to avoid both areas. Being West of the Mississippi is safer than being East of the Mississippi. In future maps we will see an inland sea develop along the Mississippi with great destruction around this area.

The center points of the primary hot zones include the San Andrea's Fault and associated faults as far East as Nevada and the New Madrid Fault along the Mississippi. These are very serious fault areas that will let go sometime in the near future.

Tsunami/Flood Zones

The map below shows probable areas where tsunami or flood is most likely to occur. This is an official US Navy map indicting the new coastlines of America sometime in the future.

Future US Navy Map

You will notice that the drop of large land areas in becoming inland seas in the US matches with the major earthquake center points indicted in the map above.

Nuclear Fall-out Zones

Nuclear fall-out is one of the most destructive forces as it is very difficult to escape its long-term destruction to life. It cannot be seen and it is best policy to avoid the areas where it is most likely to occur as the optimum solution.

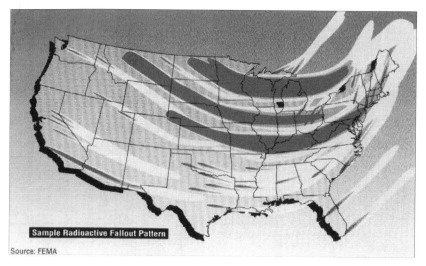

Sample Radioactive Fallout Pattern
Source: FEMA

In the two maps provided, it shows north central of the US as the most destructive areas for nuclear fall-out. This is largely due to an extensive number of nuclear silos and missile bases existing in these locations. Many of these are now being de-commissioned in exchange for Star-wars type nuclear capabilities.

FALLOUT HIGH RISK AREAS
NUCLEAR ATTACK PLANNING BASE - 1990

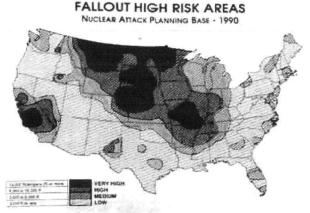

The second map above identifies fallout patterns from nuclear test sites that if destroyed would spread nuclear fall-out to the East of their locations. If you are living near of the dotes on this map, get out and move to an area that is less likely to be destructive to you, your family and friends.

I live in central Colorado just south of the fall-out path running through CO. However, the winds over the Rockies are very unpredictable so it is hard to estimate the final direction of winds pushing over the fifty 14,000 foot mountains along the Continental Divide.

Combined Disaster Zone Maps
Both the maps to follow are projections of dangerous areas and safe areas based on many criteria including nuclear, earthquake zones, tsunami/flood areas with other issues that would challenge sustaining life. The dark areas are to be avoided in the following two maps.

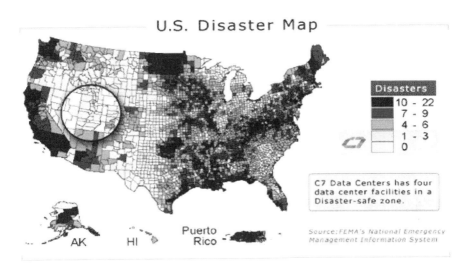

All of the maps presented are best guess approaches by experts from various fields. These are government maps and should be taken very seriously. Now let's take a look at some prophetic maps or what I call dream maps.

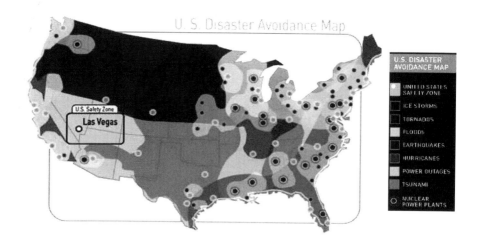

Invasion Map

This is a dream map below so I thought I would put it here since a safe place is where invading forces are less likely to transverse.

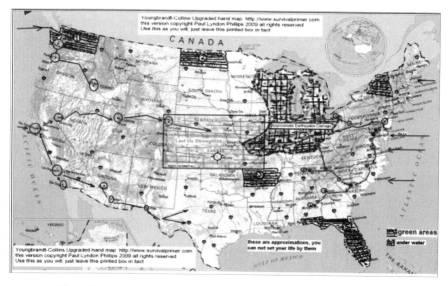

This dream map shows two primary entry points. In the West Coast, there is entry in California and the other in Seattle.

The CA invasion splits with one line running along the Mexico border and tho other through the center of the US. I-70 is the likely road for an invasion through the center of the US although this map has the invasion going East through southern Wyoming. The Western invasion seems to target the wheat and corn belt located mostly in Kansas. If you can control the food source, you will control the world.

The invasion through the East Coast covers most of the populated areas in the East and still ends in Kansas. The NAFTA highway is thought to be the intended transportation network for the coming food distribution draining the US of its primary grain food source to feed the NWO armies deployed around the world.

Prophetic Maps

We will review a number of prophetic maps that are available on the internet to compare them to try to identify what might be considered safe areas in America to go to when the economy fails and the NWO takes over American completely.

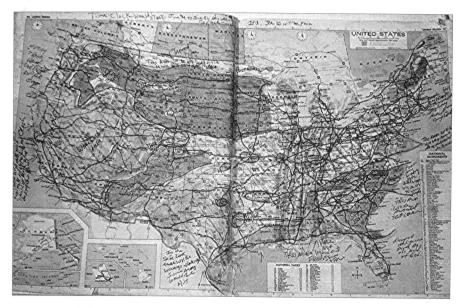

Disaster Map One

The map above was from a dream by another prophet – not sure who – still researching this. I cannot verify any of this but present it because it seems to have much detail. The darker gray is considered safe areas however the gray area along the central Canadian border is also the site for major nuclear facilities and shows up on the nuclear fall-out as not a safe place unless you stay in the Rockies which is West of these facilities. Neither would I suggest being on the East Coast as this is subject to Tsunamis.

What I do agree with is the SW Colorado and NE Arizona are safe areas. This area is confirmed as safe by all other maps. It also shows the destruction or disappearing of the Mississippi basin centering over the New Madrid fault area.

The big SOON coming cataclysmic event for America is the New Madrid Fault giving way. This in itself will cause massive Tsunamis – some 1000 feet tall hitting the coastal shores of Africa, Europe and the upper East Coast of America. All that may be untouched by this event is the lands West of the Mississippi and the higher elevations of the Appalachian and Adirondack mountains.

Disaster Map Two

■ Disappeared ▨ Much Devastation

This dream map above is also from another prophet and shows similar areas of disaster and safety. I find this dream map does not follow the geography of America's mountains and should be compared with other dream maps for clarification.

The idea that Texas disappeared along with whole States on the West Coast and the East Coast is hard to believe. It does however confirm the center points of the expected disaster areas. It is just more severe than most other maps.

Disaster Map Three

The next map below seems very suspect since it shows destruction areas very different from the other maps in this section. What it does show is the Pacific encroaching as far as the Western Slope of Colorado. It also shows a new mountain range emerge East of Colorado in Kansas.

There has been a number of people that show the encroachment of the Pacific as far as Colorado with this area of America dropping down below sea level. The gray in this map is now under water whereas the white is possible safe areas from this cataclysmic event.

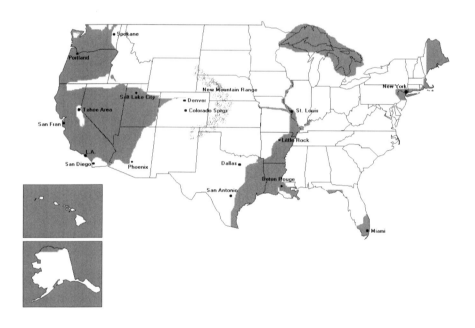

Disaster Map Four

This map was created by a Dr. Chet Snow and seems to follow similar lines of water destruction to the other disaster maps already provided. This maps make it clear that both the West Coast and East Coast are destroyed by Tsunami and may remain partially under water.

MISSISSIPPI RIVER
50+ miles wide

PROJECTED AREAS OF DESTRUCTION
BY WATER   1995-1999

PRIMARY
SECONDARY

Disaster Map Five

This map below again follows the line of other disaster maps. In all cases the East coastal lands are gone with most or all of Florida.

What is interesting in this map is the emergence of new land to the South East of the North American continent. This is expected to occur by the Templars and other secret religious groups as Atlantis rises up from the bottom of the sea to again become a place of sacred worship. The remaining evidence for the existence of Atlantis is the various roads and man-made mesas found just below sea level off of the island of Bimini.

It is believed the small island of Bimini will become the top of a high mountain as the New Madrid Fault gives way with the eastern plate of the US sliding to the south-east into the sea and thus lifting up the plate below Bimini Island and making it a high mountain.

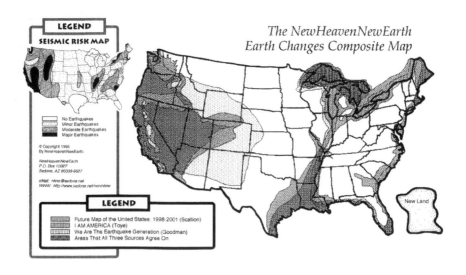

Disaster Map Six

This map below is more radical than the rest but does seem to follow the lines of destruction that you will see in the map to follow created by the UN. It shows only the Appalachian mounties in higher elevations surviving East of the Mississippi with the NE of the US still intact around the Adirondacks.

future map of united states

Disaster Map Seven

The following map is also radical and provides for the rise of land that would be the ancient Atlantis as in disaster map six.

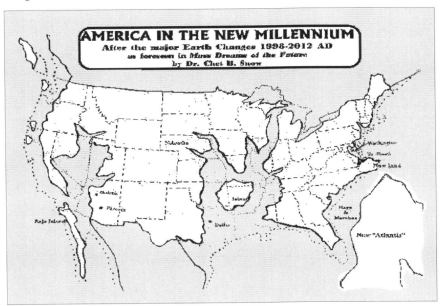

Abbot David's Disaster Map

The following map is from a dream (or benevolent abduction?) I had on the 11 of August 2011. What I dreamed is much the same as many of the other maps except for the Alien Andromadan presence of their ships in this dream.

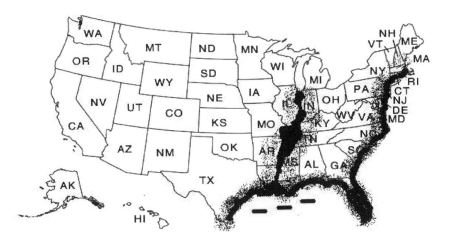

I was aboard the far left Andromadan Mother ship located over the gulf of Mexico as I saw the Madrid Fault let loose and fail resulting in what you see above in my dream map.

What is a bit different in my dream map is a larger inland sea in the area of the New Madrid Fault area. I did not see the West Coast in this dream so I do not know what its condition was as a result of the fall of the Eastern US Continental plate.

It is believed by many writers the Eastern part of the North American Continental plate will actually slide into the sea to the South and East and cause an uplifting of the remains of what was once Atlantis in the Caribbean..

Just off shore of Bimini Island is where large stone paved roads and walls have been discovered and is said to be the primary remains of this once advanced cultural cities according to the Templars and other researchers. It is also believed by them that it will arise again to become a cultural center for the NWO religion. No doubt this will occur as the New Madrid Fault occurs to force it up above sea level to again be inhabited.

NWO Map of the Future

This map below is a very foretelling map created by the Biodiversity people who are a NWO front of the Illuminati. What is amazing is that the biodiversity reserves and corridors (in dark shade) to the East of the Mississippi are very sparse – almost non-existent. When asked why they did not complete the map, they said that they have not gotten to it yet. I do not believe this in the least. It is intentional.

You will notice only the higher elevation of the Appalachian Mountains are set aside for biodiversity. This may indicate they expect the Eastern seaboard as far as the Mississippi to sink as a result of earthquakes only leaving the Appalachian mountains above sea level to exist along with the Adirondacks.

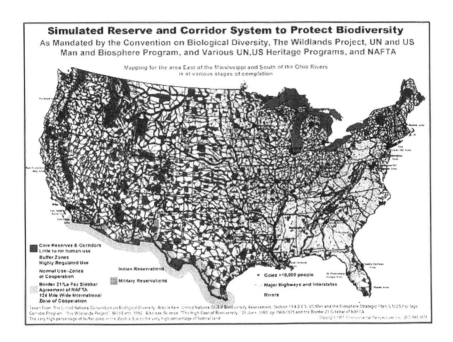

Where Are the Safe Places

The reality is you are safe if you are sensitive to the Holy Spirit and are being obedient to his leading for you and your family as to where you should live in the coming difficulties.

However, never should the excuse be, "I cannot afford to move" be a response. If this is your excuse, you are not being sensitive to the leading of the Holy Spirit but are being led by fear and unbelief.

Seeing into the Future

If you could see into the future and knew your family were to die two weeks from now unless you make the right decision today, would you quit your job and move immediately? Most would say yes. If you wait until you can see all that is being prophesied coming to pass in reality, it is then too late.

It is time to get your family together and pray together about all this and seek to come into agreement. If certain members, a husband or a wife, will not accept what the prophets are saying in these last days, you should still do what you can to prepare and be ready.

Be Prepared

Minimally put together emergency pack-sacks of provisions and items what would be needed if you have to escape your home and city quickly. The areas that I personally have identified as safe are the Smokey Mountains around the Asheville area in NC, the Adirondacks around the Winter Park area in NY, the Rockies in S. Colorado and Arizona and North West Arkansas in the Ozarks.

There is no real safe place on the West Coast that I know of. In all cases, it is the mountains that are important providing they are not subject to volcanic eruption, explosion or major earthquakes.

The mountains around Yellowstone are now under watch as the ground is rising from underground pressure suggesting a possible catastrophic volcanic eruption. The Yellowstone volcano is so huge, it would wipe out most of the States East of it with ash blowing from a massive eruption.

Some say it would be so massive it could create a new ice age but this is not supported in the books of prophecy for the end times in the Bible.   Most of the volcanic West Coast mountains are not considered trustingly dormant due to the constantly colliding plate tectonics. You should consider them all active volcanoes.

Proposed Safe Places

Pray about all that has been presented in this chapter and please make this a very high priority. What I have attempted to do here is provide a map below that identifies what appears to be safe areas from volcanic eruptions, earthquake, tsunami, hostile military invasion as US/UN forces and nuclear fall-out.

These areas identified below in black may not be the only areas of safety as it is the Holy Spirit and the Angels who will ultimately make a place safe. However, relocating to or near these safe area places assures a better chance of survival if you have no other leading. The key over and above a safe place is being with safe people you can trust who are not globalists or NWO socialists.

Stay away from living on land that has HOA's (development or neighborhood associations) as these are by their very nature socialist where a few people tell the rest how they should live. I have not found one HOA that is not doing the work of the NWO in preparing its members to let others tell them how to live. My map of safe places is provided here.

Five Safe Areas Identified

The five areas in shaded black are the central areas of these safety zones. The Montana safe areas are hidden valleys with water sources within the Rocky Mountains and these follow the high Rockies down to Colorado and then to the 4-corners area.

The 4-corners safe area is largely within the Native reservations and the safety here is if there can be a covenant re-established between the Native Americans and a remnant of Whites who hold to the Hebrew Christian faith and practice.

The Arkansas safe area seems to be near the New Madrid Fault but due to the height and rock structures under this area, it is considered a safe area in the Ozarks.

The Appalachian Mountains safe area centers around Ashville in North Carolina. This land may become the center of government for the new Eastern American country after the New Madrid Fault goes. It would be like finding a safe place in Nazi Germany in the middle of Berlin. Go there only if the Holy Spirit leads you to do so.

Hawaii as a safe area is high on the Big Island away from the shore line – higher the better as tsunami waves will be washing over the islands without mercy.

The New York safe area is in the Adirondacks mountains near the Lake Placid area and to the north in these mountains. The higher elevations are necessary to avoid a massive killer tsunami that will run up the St. Lawrence river and wipe out all in its path up into the Great Lakes area.

Heeding the Warnings

It is clear we have had warnings from the study of nature, biblical prophecy, political-economic researchers, and modern prophets to prepare us for the difficulties that will soon come upon the earth.

These signs are before us to suggest we have a very short time to be prepared for what is coming. Will you listen and be ready? Will you save your family? Will you choose to be a child of YHWH and not a child of Mammon and the world system?

Chapter 2: Executive Orders Suspend Constitution
Executive Orders

Numerous Executive Orders signed into law by US presidents have paved the way for a complete takeover of all resources in the US by a crises government working through the FEMA agency of the US Government. The Orders that take away your independence secured by the US Constitution are as follows.

EXECUTIVE ORDER 10990 allows the government to take over all modes of transportation and control of highways and seaports.

EXECUTIVE ORDER 10995 allows the government to seize and control the communication media.

EXECUTIVE ORDER 10997 allows the government to take over all electrical power, gas, petroleum, fuels and minerals.

EXECUTIVE ORDER 10998 allows the government to take over all food resources and farms.

EXECUTIVE ORDER 11000 allows the government to mobilize civilians into work brigades under government supervision.

EXECUTIVE ORDER 11001 allows the government to take over all health, education and welfare functions.

EXECUTIVE ORDER 11002 designates the Postmaster General to operate a national registration of all persons.

EXECUTIVE ORDER 11003 allows the government to take over all airports and aircraft, including commercial and private aircraft.

EXECUTIVE ORDER 11004 allows the Housing and Finance Authority to relocate communities, build new housing with public funds, designate areas to be abandoned, and establish new locations for populations.

EXECUTIVE ORDER 11005 allows the government to take over railroads, inland waterways and public storage facilities.

EXECUTIVE ORDER 11051 specifies the responsibility of the Office of Emergency Planning and gives authorization to put all Executive Orders into effect in times of increased international tensions and economic or financial crisis.

EXECUTIVE ORDER 11310 grants authority to the Department of Justice to enforce the plans set out in Executive Orders, to institute industrial support, to establish judicial and legislative liaison, to control all aliens, to operate penal and correctional institutions, and to advise and assist the President.

EXECUTIVE ORDER 11049 assigns emergency preparedness function to federal departments and agencies, consolidating 21 operative Executive Orders issued over a fifteen year period.

EXECUTIVE ORDER 11921 allows the Federal Emergency Preparedness Agency to develop plans to establish control over the mechanisms of production and distribution, of energy sources, wages, salaries, credit and the flow of money in U.S. financial institution in any undefined national emergency. It also provides that when a state of emergency is declared by the President, Congress cannot review the action for six months. The Federal Emergency Management Agency has broad powers in every aspect of the nation.

President Takes Your Food

The heart of these Presidential Orders secure the complete control of all resources in the US needed for life. Those who are 'preppers' in preparing for the collapse of the US are subject to these Executive Orders and if they have reserves of food and fuel, these will be confiscated and redistributed. It is my understanding that individuals and families will only be allowed to store a 30 day supply of resources of any kind including food, water and fuel.

Obama has recently signed into law the following Executive Order that further suspends the US Constitution. Also included in this Order is the liberty given to the US Government to implement Martial Law even during peace time without cause.

Under this [Obama] order the heads of these cabinet level positions; Agriculture, Energy, Health and Human Services, Transportation, Defense and Commerce can take food, livestock, fertilizer, farm equipment, all forms of energy, water resources, all forms of civil transportation (meaning any vehicles, boats, planes), and any other materials, including construction materials from wherever they are available. This is probably why the government has been visiting farms with GPS devices, so they know exactly where to go when they turn this one on.

Martial Law Anytime Now

The stage is set for the US Government to take over all assets including your personal assets to redistribute as they think necessary. This is a drastic move toward totalitarian socialism or a form of fascism. You will have no recourse at Law to keep anything you have purchased, grown, made and stored to prepare yourself for more difficult times such as will occur with a complete economic collapse.

With Obama's EO, implementing Martial Law does not need the justification of an economic collapse or catastrophe to be implemented – it can be done anytime by the US President without any reason whatsoever. The confiscation of all guns will to occur just before or immediately after Martial Law is implemented. The current Obama government has made it clear he will not leave one gun in the hands of any civilian American if this is possible.

I have read that a trucker checked his load he was carrying for the US Government and found his 50' semi loaded full with thousands of 'Martial Law' signs he was hauling to different parts of the country.

Do not think this is just a conspiracy theory to be disregarded. There are compelling facts to prove the US Government is planning to implement Martial Law very soon and all is now ready for it to occur.

It will likely occur before the end of the current presidential term of Obama.   When this occurs, presidential elections will be suspended under Martial Law and thus make Obama the first US dictator serving as a pawn under the 'New World Order' global government.

Chapter 3: How to Survive in the Wilderness
Optimum Dwelling

After living in the high Rockies at 10,000 feet for the last 5 years, the idea of living in a tent in winter is not appealing to me except perhaps if a properly designed tipi or yurt with wood stove. I would not even want to live in a conventional travel trailer as these seldom can be heated sufficiently in the winter to stay warm in below zero temperatures with the supplied heating systems.

The key objective for mountain emergency survival is to keep the wind, snow and rain off and have substantial insulation to hold the heat in. In addition, there is a need to cook and heat water only using fuels that are readily available for free from where you are located. Propane or methane fuels cannot be harvested from a tree unless you are skilled in wood-gas production.

Heating Concerns

It is also a fact that the bigger your living space is, the more it will cost in time or money to keep it heated. In the days of the Mountainman, if he were able to keep the temperature of his self-built cabin up to 40 degrees when the outside was 20 below zero, he was happy.

For the modernized American, if it is not 70 plus degrees in their dwelling throughout the winter, they are in abject misery. So the question remains, "how much space do you need?" How about space for two people? How about a family of 5 or 7?

Size of Dwelling

All that is really needed is a place to sleep and cook that is protected from the weather. A bed can be 2.5' by 6' for most people - larger for some Americans. This is about 15 square feet. For cooking and heating, perhaps another 15 square feet. This suggests about 30 square feet or about a 5' by 6' area per person minimally.

Living in the wild should encourage one to get outside as much as possible properly dressed to enjoy the great winter outside and to hunt and gather food. The dwelling is mainly for sleep and cooking and to get out of adverse weather. This is the way of the mountainman.

Add another 20 square feet for each additional person and we have about 30 sq feet for one, 50 sq. feet for 2, 110 sq. feet for 5 and 150 sq. feet for 7. My construction trailer I have lived in during the winter is 350 sq. feet in size. This is more than enough room for a family of seven who have adapted to the outdoor life of the mountains. Using bunks adds even more floor space for living.

The point of this exercise is to realistically calculate the optimal size of a dwelling based on actual necessity and not based upon the status quo expectancy of the spoiled and extravagant American. The key here is to reduce the energy needed to heat the dwelling and thus the work load of the primary provider.

Earth Shelter Dwelling

The best choice in methods and materials for a dwelling is one that is partially submerged in the soil like in a hill side with only high widows and the roof exposed.

The roof would then have 2 or more feet of soil on top for insulation. This is called an Earth Shelter where the heat of the earth which is about 40-50 degrees 6 feet down and deeper is used to help heat your dwelling and keep the heat in on very cold days.

It is also cooler during the hot summer because the earth temperature does not change much though summer and winter.

The construction process is to dig a hole into a hill side or straight down about 5-8 feet and then build a very strong timber (log) frame with heavy walls to withstand the in-pressing weight of the soil. It needs to be waterproofed below ground level and this can be done with roll polyester sheeting and roofing compounds. Elastomeric roofing compounds that are painted on hard surfaces work very well and have a long life.

An easy form of construction is a post and beam approach with very close posts and heavy 3/4" wood ply applied in two layers or 2" thick framing lumber used as outside walls for closing in between the posts and beams. Many books are available as well as on-line instructions for building earth shelters with many great innovations.

Water and Sanitation

Since your floor is underground more than 6 foot already, you might consider digging below the floor level and adding a 200 gallon fresh water tank if a winter flowing stream is not near by. You may also use 55 gallon plastic barrels for water - perhaps 4 of them for you water needs. Being buried in the earth, the water in the tanks will not freeze.

For sanitation, the traditional outhouse is still the easiest solution. Grey water can be used for growing plants if you build on a hill facing to the south and have the south side of your earth home windowed as a green house for growing food in the winter. The best mountain tub/shower I have used is a small galvanized stock tank just large enough to stand or sit in. A shower curtain is optional if privacy is desired.

Food

Many want to prepare for the coming crises by having a variety of foods available to them by canning and preserving summer produce and meats. I have no issue with this but I prefer to keep my meat on the hoof and harvest it as I need it.

For veggies, store roots when available and sprout seeds for greens when needed. For starch, rice is a good choice with brown rice being more nutritious. Keep you menu simple and efficient then add to it as you have the time and the resources.

For storing food, I like sun drying the best – especially for fruits. For meats, preserving the meat by smoking is my favorite. Drying and smoking makes for a very light and nutritious food should one have to travel on foot and carry their food with them. Stews using dried veggies and meats is always a good staple for the winter months. Dried fruits taste like candy.

Can't Afford to Build

In the case where you cannot afford to build and don't have property to build on, the alternative is for a mobile dwelling. If you were not wanting to acquire a Survival Wagon from us, you could take an old travel trailer, gut it, insulate it better and then install a 2 burner wood cook stove and bunks for living.

With a wood stove, you must have some ventilation so carbon monoxide does not accumulate in the trailer and kill you while you sleep. Add extra insulation in the floor and ceiling if possible. Develop a water storage system that uses 5 gallon water jugs. Automatic water tank systems common to travel trailers are prone to freeze up in sub zero temperatures and stay that way until spring thaw. Keep a big pot on the stove for hot water to use as needed.

Tools

You can build all that is mentioned above with just hand tools but I would recommend at least having a good gas powered chain saw for building your earth shelter and cutting fire wood. I would still have a good tree saw or back saw as a backup for log cutting.

Add to this a brace and bits, large slick (2-3" wide chisel), froe for making shingles, various axes, small sledge, draw knives, wood saws, screw drivers, chisels, measuring rule, hammers and misc hardware. I am a blacksmith so this helps in making hardware and odd tools if I need something in particular. I would still have misc. hinges, claps and nails/screws of various sizes on hand rather then try to make them.

I would guess you are now ready to build your survival solution to be better prepared for the coming economic crash of American society. The first thing to do is to sit down and make a list of your resources to know what you have and what you will have to get to be ready. It is always better to be ready before calamity comes than try to be ready after it comes. It just makes better sense to be ready now.

Chapter 4: Salt for Survival and Trade

Thanks to Pauly who is a friend of mine for this chapter since he told me I had to put this in here or 'die the death'. He was joking... I think. Salt! We can't live without it. In a matter of a few weeks with no salt, your body starts to shut down and in time you will die without having a source of salt in your diet.

Salt is a preservative for food and is used to enhance the taste in the foods that we eat. Salt has in past history been a very good commodity of trade with many acquiring great wealth in producing salt from sea water or mining salt. As the economy collapses, salt will again become a commodity of trade and vital for survival. If you can choose to live near a natural salt source and can secure this source from marauders, you will have a good product for trade after the collapse.

Barter will become the method of commerce and salt will be a necessity for the thousands who have not had enough foresight to make all of the preparations needed for their future survival.

Salt is also used for medical purposes. It has been used as a disinfectant and is mixed with healing herbs to better draw out their healing essences to be used in poultices and other remedies.

So thank you Pauly for inspiring this chapter and may salt never get in your eye as you stand too close behind those who for some religious reason toss salt behind them as they mumble some prayer of protection from the evils of this world.

Chapter 5: Dream – Toxic Water in America
War Across America

In the early morning of the 24th of February, I saw in a dream a great war in America. I saw destruction everywhere with the effects of nuclear, chemical and biological weapons being used against the American people by invading forces.

I then saw the condition of the water over the face of the land. There was little potable water to be had at any price. The war in American had made all of the easily accessible water toxic with nuclear fall-out, toxic chemicals used in battle and biological weapons. I saw death everywhere with dead animals and people scattered along the shores of streams, lakes and reservoirs.

Cost of Water

I then heard a man cry out and tell the price of good water. He said it would cost $25,000 to fill a small 2-man bunker with ice. He said this ice that he was selling had been mined from deep within ancient glaciers. This was the only potable water that was considered to be safe to drink after the war. I then awoke.

Wondering what the price per gallon would be for safe drinking water after the coming war in America, I made the following calculations:

Bunker size:	8' by 8' by 7' high = 448 cu. ft.
Convert ft³. to gal.	1 cu. ft. = 7.48 gal.
Calculate total gal.	7.48 X 448 = 3351 gal.
20% loss due to ice	3351 X .80 = 2680 gal.
Bulk price per gal.	25,000 / 2680 = $9.33 per gal.

Keep in mind this $9.33 a gallon is a bulk price when buying 2680 gallons of frozen glacier ice. In smaller quantities, it is very reasonable to expect that water will sell for over $20 per gallon or even much higher in more remote areas after the coming war.

Toxic Wells

As it rains, the chemical toxins and nuclear fall-out will leach into the soil and eventually get into the water table making water from wells dangerous to drink. Filtering may work for chemical toxins but not for nuclear fall-out.

I believe this dream is a warning given to us by YHWH to be prepared for very high prices for water. If we can secure a water source that will not be effected by nuclear fall-out, chemical or biological weapons, then we would have a very barterable commodity and a precious life sustaining resource.

Chapter 6: Rednecks Won't Make It
Protecting your Property

I have lived for the past 5 years in the high mountains of Colorado at about 10,000 foot elevation near Hartsel, Colorado. Occasionally I go to the only social gathering place in town called the saloon. It has recently changed its name from HOB to Highline Cafe. HOB stood for Hateful Old Bitch in identifying the former owner of the dive.

Often the topic of discussion comes up about the coming take over of America by the US shadow government and the taking away of the rights afforded to citizens by the US Constitution. I hear over and over again how these Rocky Mountain Rednecks (not referring to a species of pheasant here) will sit on their hill side with their trusty deer rifle and shoot anyone that tries to take away what is theirs.

Gunships and Armored Vehicles

I usually will tell them just as a point of interest that it  will take far more than a deer rifle to stop the potential assault against you and your property.

When they come to you with missile loaded helicopter gunships and armored vehicles, your deer rifle will be about as effective as a pea shooter against a wild bull. They may just opt to blow you and your house to oblivion with a guided missile. There will be no concern for your rights by then since the US Constitution will have already been suspended under Martial Law.

I once read about 10 years go that there are over 60,000 stealth helicopter gunships stuffed away in bunkers across the US waiting for the time of a Constitutional revolt. I would expect there are much more now in reserve as we approach a political-economic collapse in the US.

No Privacy

The internet is now fully monitored by the US shadow government. Expected privacy is but a mere illusion. If you have ever written an email with a negative view of the current trend in government related to the removal of Constitutional liberties, you are on their 'watch' list. If you have used credit cards or checks to buy bulk foods, you are on their watch list.

If you have bought precious metals and this can be traced when buying from a US approved companies, you are on the watch list. If you have a registered gun in your possession, you are on their watch list. If you have subscribed to any organization by mail or the internet who opposes the US shadow government takeover of the US or even just clicked and spent time on a web site that has this material, you are on their watch list. If you have any criminal record – if more than a few parking tickets, you are on their watch list.

Midnight Removal

For those who have used public information systems (internet, mail, telephone, radio) to incite the preparation of an organized resistance of arms against any force that would undermine or threaten the liberties of the US Constitution, you are on their high priority hit list.

The hit list has the names and location of people who may/will be arrested by Special Forces trained teams in the middle of the night possibly <u>before</u> Martial law is implemented. This is to prevent such a person from joining with others to become a real armed threat. There will be no warning or sign before this happens from the regular press or anywhere. It will just quietly happen one night when most of the world is asleep.

Who Can Resist

There is only one kind of soldier that may be able to make a difference and that is a well trained sniper who knows the art of stealth and can completely disappear into the Rocky Mountain wilderness. Since any Constitutional resistance will be against armored ground vehicles and armored helicopter gunships filled with advanced military electronics, the rifles will need to have great power and shoot accurately over very long distances such as common with the 50 caliber sniper rifles.

A silencer is suggested since military electronics can now triangulate the source of a gunshot sound and respond with a full arsenal of weapons that will leave just a hole in the ground where you once were sitting.

This is definitely not a Redneck approach of waiting for the bad guys to come to your home as you sit on your front porch in your rocking chair drinking a beer with your rifle in hand. It is a highly trained approach and only a few will be able to make the grade. For the rest of us, it is advised we get out of 'Dodge' into the mountains to a safe place we have already prepared before the proverbial manure of Martial Law hits the fan.

When Martial Law is enforced, most of the access roads will be closed to traffic imprisoning the residents of the cities and local communities. You will not be allowed to leave. This means if you are living in a city and have a place in the country prepared as an escape, you will not be allowed to leave the city to go to your safe place.

It is well known that the US is training UN forces in large numbers of over 5000 in a group on American soil to assist in so-called "peace keeping" activities in the US when Martial Law is decreed. 5000 Russians were seen in training in NC in the mountains just a few years ago. The US has and is training Chinese, Russians and East Germans who would have no second thoughts about shooting an American. The fact is these counties generally hate Americans and shooting one trying to escape the city would be a pleasure for them.

If you consider yourself a redneck American, I suggest you take what I have presented her seriously. Study into the art of stealth, wilderness survival and learn to shoot accurately from great distances. Become a one-man army as a sniper to keep the NWO armies in fear of where your next shot will find its target.

Chapter 7: Dream – Slavery of the Fuel Economy
The Dream

In the early morning of the 27th of February 2013, I had a dream where I was driving across America in a small pickup pulling a shepherd's wagon as a camper. I was on a mission in stopping at safe places across America to bring hope and encouragement to the remnant Church in hiding from the antichrist regime then in power.

I looked down at my feet in the pickup and notice my gas pedal was colored blood red. I noticed the brake pedal was also red but of a much lighter color.

I wondered about this while still dreaming, "Why was my gas pedal bright red?" I then heard a voice in the dream that said, "Since you were using the fuel supplied by the Antichrist regime also known as the New World Order (NWO), you are under their power and the faster and farther you drove, using their provided gas even through you bought it, the more you were adding to their right to demand your blood in the Courts of Heaven." I was dumbfounded at hearing this.

Breaking slowed down this process somewhat but not the final outcome of this judgment by Satan. Thus the reason for the lighter red on the brake pedal but it was still red.

I realized while still dreaming that the more I traveled to bring life to the remnant Church, the more I was heaping judgment upon myself where Satan will demand my blood because I was using their provided energy to travel and by buying it, agreed to their terms of use. It is assumed by this time, the Regime will require a vow of fealty to Satan's government before you can buy or sell fuel – or use their manufactured fuel at all.

Do Not Use Satan's Resources

As I was beginning to awaken, I began to pray about this dream. I was further shown that the resources that are to be used by the remnant Church in hiding cannot come from the resources of Satan's government. They must come from nature directly or provided by YHWH supernaturally. Even stealing the fuel from the NWO will bring us under their right of judgment.

This is a hard truth to accept considering Americas sense of just jumping in a car and going wherever they want to without much thought of who they are becoming the servant of in using their resources. Gas stations, refineries and oil wells are all heavily controlled by government regulations and we as the people can only use this form of energy by agreeing to all of the terms of the purchase agreement. This is a physical and spiritual fact.

Churches Source is Nature

Therefore based on this dream, our fuel and energy must come directly from nature or supernaturally. If we can understand this truth, we will save ourselves from great distress in the future.

If we live fully outside of the controls of the now emerging antichrist NWO government by not using their fuel and other 'manufactured' resources, YHWH become our sole provider and we then remain under his full protection from the evil hand of the antichrist regime. It is seen in scripture that the great dragon who is Satan will aggressively and relentlessly pursue the true remnant Church and murder all he can find of those who have held to the true faith in YHWH.

Travel Resources

If travel is required, what are the alternatives to gas powered vehicles?

For near distance travel, there is the horse and the mule. I was just given a mule. I said to the Lord when I was offered this 4 year old mule that I was not ready to care for mule due to limited finances. I then realized that my timing is not God's timing and my sense of readiness is not his requirement of readiness.

Secondly, the cars I have been able to afford over the last 2 years have been lemons forcing one to pray fervently to get just a few miles in distance. I have asked the Lord why do I keep getting junk vehicles? YHWH has no problem giving us what we need and a good running car is a simple matter for God who created the universe. I can only assume YHWH is preparing me... forcing me to not be reliant upon gas powered vehicles.

Translated Travel

The other form of travel for long distance was seen in the life of Philip who was transported by YHWH to meet and Baptize the Ethiopian eunuch.

> "...And they went both down into the water, both Philip and the Eunuch; and he baptized him.
> And when they were come up out of the water, the Spirit of the Lord caught away Philip, that the Eunuch saw him no more; and he went on his way rejoicing.

But Philip was found at Azotus."   Acts 8:26-40.

Here we see Philip at the River Jordan and then suddenly he was instantly whisked away by the Holy Spirit and found at Azotus. He was supernaturally transported.

The fact is we do not need to use the fuel and energy resources of the NWO but can through faith come to rely upon the resources provided by nature and YHWH who is still the uncontested creator of nature in its raw form.

To commit to only use the resources of YHWH as a means of transport will keep us protected and safe to fulfill the mission of YHWH without the demand of our blood by Satan. Choosing God's solution will keep us from pressing the blood-red gas pedal that will put us under the justified judgment of Satan.

Other Transport Options

For me this is a big step as I had three 1969 VW bajas and a converted school bus ready for transport in the mountains when the antichrist regime openly controls all fuel availability.

Sadly, I could not keep the 3 VW Bajas running reliably either and the fuel cost of the bus makes its usefulness limited. I have recently sold the 3 VW's and may after this dream convert the bus to a wood-gas fuel system that enables me to burn wood and power the Chevy 350 short block engine.

Another alternative for local transport is the bicycle. This option needs much more consideration given the message of this dream. Bicycles can be powered (assisting the human peddler) with solar powered electrical motors, compressed air motors and even a small compact wood fired steam engine. Steam powered bicycles were available in the late 1800's. More on this later in this book in chapter 26.

We will do well if we heed this message as we prepare for the difficulties of the end times that are soon to come upon us and even now is raising its ugly head in the form of economic depression, job loss and the inevitable bankruptcy of the US government implemented by President Obama.

Chapter 8: Gold or Cash
America Bankrupt

There was a time when we were on the gold standard in the US and you could at any time take you paper money down to any bank and trade it in for gold or silver. This ceased during the Great Depression when the US went bankrupt and starting printing more money than there was gold and sliver to back it up. This money was then distributed to start massive employment projects such as dams, highways and other infrastructures.

Our currency at that time became fiat money that had no real value behind it and thus began to loose buying power through inflation. As more money was printed, the less value it had. What you could buy in the 40's for $1.00 would cost you at least $20.00 now.

This means that the value of the dollar is now worth only 5 cents on the dollar. This is not considered hyper inflation however as the value of the dollar continues to decrease and the Feds just keep printing more money to be able to pay their debts to other countries. However, there comes a time when other countries will no longer accept the dollar to pay trade debts and hyper inflation begins. We are at this juncture now.

China has been buying our debt for the last few years and recently has resisted this in demanding gold as collateral for the debt. It is rummered that billions of dollars in gold has been secretly shipped to China to entice them to continue to buy our debt owed to them and to other countries. This cannot go on forever and the day of reckoning is near

It is not known just how much gold remains in the US such as at Fort Knox. Some suggest the holdings are no more than just gold plated lead put there for show to give Americans on tour a false sense of economic security.

You will notice that gold buyers are everywhere offering to buy your gold jewelry with fiat money to then sell this gold at a good price to the US government when the US fiat money known as the US Dollar becomes completely worthless.

Amero Coming Soon

The feds will then use this gold to further extend our credit to China and other countries in buying down our debt. I would expect this spiraling decline will not continue through much beyond 2013 when a new money standard may be introduced.

When this happens, whatever US dollars you have saved will have little or no value except to trade in for buying credit in the new money system. Once this happens, you will not have the ability to buy or sell unless you agree to use the new money system.

The new money system is being called the Amero and will effectively remove the borders between Canada, the US and Mexico.

Borders Unprotected

You may wonder why the US is not protecting our southern border from Mexican invasion. The reason is Mexico will soon become a part of the new North American government as a part of the global world government.

Our resolve may be to invest in gold as a real currency that we can later use to buy and sell on a 'black market' economy separate from the Amero money system. In order for this to work, gold will have to be 'coined' into very small values of perhaps $20 units. Twenty dollars in gold is no more than a drop of sliver or gold and is difficult to handle due to its small size.

The alternative is to form co-ops of gold owners that then issue among themselves 'stock' or 'bearer bonds' that represents a portion of the gold that is secretly held and protected by the co-op. The question will then be where will the gold be secretly kept and protected?

Templar Banks

In the past, the Templars provided a similar service to many and due to their honesty, were trusted throughout Europe. A noble would give to the Templars a chest of gold in Europe and then travel to the Middle East for a pilgrimage. Upon arriving, he could then go to the Templars there and request the same amount of gold back less a usury fee for the service. This would prevent his loosing his fortune to thieves and pirates during the trip or having to carry very heavy chests of gold that would slow down the travel.

Co-op Banking

It may be that the underground Church becomes the keepers of the gold for the members of the various congregations. I am encouraging the creation of a CO-OP here in the mountains of Colorado in South Park.

The CO-OP would buy bulk foods, feed, machines, tools, or anything based on member orders and then distribute the order when it arrived in the area. Along with this would be a Barter Board where locals can post what they have to trade, what they think the value is, contact information and what they are looking for. This could be a Craigslist kind of system but very local to the area.

Co-op Schools

In addition to this would be a school that teaches homesteading in the LIFE systems. Lodging for sub zero temperatures and 140 MPH winds, Industry in generating income or barter value from local resources, Food and sanitation systems that are efficient in high elevation climates and efficient low-cost alternative Energy systems in capturing the energy of the wind, geothermal, solar and water power.

The fact remains that we are at the precipice of an economic collapse in America. Gold is better than cash since it has a real value. More valuable than gold will be food, water, shelter, heat and transport. I suggest all have some gold or silver stored for the future but more invested in food, tools and simple machines that are powered from alternative energy resources.

Chapter 9: Mobile Resistance
Being Hunted

If the true church continues to be outspoken against abortion, the stealing away of US Constitutional liberties, the socialist agenda in the undermining of the institution of the family, many Christians will become identified as domestic terrorists by the US Government.

As this occurs - actually has been don already, you will find yourself on the hit list as an alleged domestic terrorist. Your right to own property will be canceled by the US Government with all you assets confiscated. This means houses, vehicles, stock investments and other assets will no longer be available to you.

In addition, there is a good chance you will be incarcerated and held without trail as is the current procedure signed into law by Presidential Executive Orders and the various co-called Patriot Acts. Now there is a current government move to establish a new court system that is separate from both civil and federal courts to address foreign and domestic terrorism in the US.

This new court will not be connected with citizen rights of the US Constitution and their judgments cannot be challenged. Both foreign and domestic terrorists will be given to this court and Constitutional protections will not be available to persons subjected to this court. It will have an autonomy similar to the IRS courts and the Child Protection Enforcement courts that exist today.

Once knowing you are on the Federalist radar and will soon be investigated as a possible domestic terrorist, you may have only a short time to decide how you will prepare for an inevitable confrontation. If taken into custody and detained, you will be subject to the outcome of the terrorist courts and the approach will likely be 'guilty until proven innocent'. This is a court against ideologies and not any proven action. You will have no defense.

The alternative is to not be around when the Federalist police come but be elsewhere without a forwarding address. Even if you have a vehicle, it may be identified with an APB sent out to locate you and the vehicle. One who is outspoken on moral issues in the US should also have a plan to disappear quickly if needed.

If one has a family, this can be very challenging. Should one decide to live alone for the sake of their wife and children and choose to live separately or should a patriot try to bring their family with them in the escape.

How will you travel? Will you go to a hidden place in the US or abroad? What route? Where will you stay? Where will you find food and heating? Who can you trust?

I understand that there are numerous UN sovereign land parcels within the borders of the US. This means it is not under the jurisdiction of the Federal Government but under the sovereign control of the United Nations like a foreign embassy on US soil. I have yet to find these parcels but it posses an interesting possibility for exile and asylum from Constitutionally illegal Federalist pursuit in the US.

If one had protection in association with a UN NGO, this may be sufficient to stay the hand of the NWO Federalists for a short time. In any case, the matter would be an issue of international law that would have to be addressed in the international courts such as found in the Hague located in the Netherlands.

Chapter 10: To Your Boats You Land Lubbers
No Place to Hide

As we approach the end times, there will be no real safe place for a Christian unless they are truly is being led by the Holy Spirit of YHWH. There is a surge among Christians in Europe to look to getting sea worthy boats to sail the 7 seas to join and assist the last day prophets that are being prepared as the 144,000 by YHWH.

The Culdee is a school of the prophets and has embraced this mandate with sailing vessels. The Culdee was originally founded by Samuel as the School of the Prophets and was brought to Ireland by Jeremiah in the 6th century BC. This school spawned the Druidic schools that fell from grace and rejected YHWH and then pursued the gods of Babylon, Egypt, India and Rome.

When the migration of the Hebrew Church came to Britain in about 36 AD, some of the Druidic schools were revived and embraced the true Messiah Y'Shua. Others remained sold into bondage to the demon-gods of Sumer, Babylon, India Egypt and Rome and warred against the Hebrew Church then called the Culdee.

The Druids lost – went underground and the Culdee became the spiritual leaders and priests of the various clans. In time, the vikings came down from the north and the Culdee were driven from their lands in Ireland and Scotland and voyaged in escape to Iceland. The vikings then came to Iceland and they went to Greenland, Nova Scotia, E. Canada and Maine.

Then the vikings came again in the 9th century and the Culdee were driven south and to the mid-west in the Americas. In all cases, the call was 'To your boats you land lubbers' and go west. Now... there is no more west to go to for the Culdee.

This history is being replayed. Since there is no west to go to, the Culdee and true Christians are being led into the high mountains and to a life at sea. The Culdee has had both traditions for 2500 years. When the mountains could no longer hide the Culdee who lived the expression of the divine Hebrew faith, the sea was the resolve as the Culdee sailed to the next place of refuge to live as the 'friends of God' and as his priests and prophets.

For the Culdee in Colorado which is located near the center of the United States, we would have to go south to the Arkansas River and follow it to the sea.

This is perhaps the beginning of the preparation for the Culdee to get ready for global evangelization by way of the 7 seas. When I was in Hawaii last, I identified a 50' steel motor sailer fishing boat that has been in dry dock for years. It has a cargo hold (originally for fish) that can carry over a ton of goods. I made initial contact with the owner to acquire the boat but could not get the financing for this optimum vessel. However, this is a need and the calling for this is now.

The Culdee as priests are now joined by the Chivalric Order of the Gate of Jerusalem who are knights trained for battle. More about this fighting Order in the last chapter of this book. When this Order fully emerges from the shows of history as a real fighting force, it will come by land and by sea as it seeks out the Nephilim to do battle.

Chapter 11: Combating Government Socialistic Terrorism

Constitution Forgotten

Socialism is undermining our US Constitution and inalienable American rights. It is seen reproducing itself in all levels of modern American society like a foreign noxious weed that kills the natural fauna. From the Federal Government, to the State, to the Counties, to the cities and even with the owners associations in subdivisions, all are now predominately socialist.

Socialism is by definition the act of infringement of the rights of the individual by legislation that is based upon the perceived benefit or rights of the masses. The government then decides what the people need – not the people. This doctrine leads to eminent domain which ultimately denies the Constitutional rights of the individual for a perceived right of the masses. Such authority has not been given to the US Government by its people.

Protecting 'Individual' Rights

In contrast, the US Constitution sought to protect the individual from the will of the masses by protecting the rights of the individual from government legislation that is based on the perceived benefit of the masses. In this article context, your ownership of land is not to be infringed upon by any government but it is yours as a sovereign right to do with as you please.

The only Constitutional constraint that historic law has imposed is if your sovereign activities create a health hazard or loss of resources for others that share common resources connected with the land such a water, air and soil (erosion), then government may get involved to bring a fair and just resolution.

The requirement of building permits and fees is an infringement if they are not solely based on health or safety. The requirement of a minimal house size and design of house by government is an infringement upon the sovereignty of the land that you own.

The demand for expensive sanitation systems is not based on health but the perceived standards of modernization. A well kept outhouse is just as healthy as the modern septic tank and leach field sanitation system that also puts the sewage into the ground - just with a lot more added water. This added water can easily allow pathogens to seep into the water table if the water table is but a few feet below the surface. A well placed outhouse located on higher ground will prevent this.

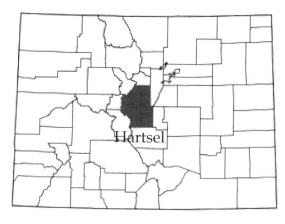

Serfs of the County Government

This trend in government control has made owners of land mere serfs and lessees of the land rather than owners. The local governments have adopted ordinances that makes them the lords over your land and you their servant.

If you do not comply, they sue you based on their rules and you pay heavy penalties or are jailed. You may also lose your land. This form of land-use terrorism needs to cease if we hope to retain anything left of the American way of life and the liberties that were secured to us by American blood as embodied in the US Constitution.

Hartsel Solution

How can we combat this rampant socialism? Here in the frontier of Hartsel in Park County, the local county government has adopted the ordinances of socialist rural Boulder and imposed it upon the struggling homesteads of the legally identified 'near-frontier' lands of South Park.

'Near frontier' status is a Federal land designation where there are virtually no improvements in the area and access to properties is by dirt road that is maintained - sometimes, by the local county road crews when they are not busy elsewhere.

Waste and 'Green' Solutions

As homesteaders, we may want/need a smaller house so we do not have to heat so much in winter yet the County requires a minimal 900 square foot dwelling. The septic system requirement is a 1000 gallon two-compartment septic tank and leach field while home-built compost toilets are forbidden. Even if you buy a manufactured compost toilet, they require the same 1000 gallon two compartment septic tack and leach field for the gray water they are deeming hazardous to the environment.

Properly disposed and filtered gray water into green houses has been done for thousands of years and is not hazardous but a good use of water resources if environmentally safe and beneficial soaps are used. Such ridicules planning ordinances are an oppressive socialist assault against the US Constitution and land-terrorism against individual American seeking to homestead frontier properties.

Ground Swell of Revolt

Many of the residents of the South Park Frontier areas are now joining together and want to fight this diabolical infringement by local government socialism.

The current plan it to take legal action as a class action suit in representing hundreds of land owners in the area against the socialist Park County government. We demand the 'Near Frontier' areas of the County be given a different set of ordinances than the rural subdivisions and towns that have electricity, well maintained paved roads and sewage utilities available at their front doors.

Further, we seek to have all County building and sanitation ordinances voted upon by the people within the County and not just decided upon in committee by a few misguided government officials and money hungry bureaucrats that create ordinances to gain more tax and permit fee revenue.

US Constitution Our Master, Not the Government People

If this works, it will provide a hands-off message to socialists in local government that we in the South Park Frontier are Patriots and we are drawing the line in the sand and do not want their socialist government intrusion into our lives. If we have to become more aggressive to convey this message as per the directives of the US Constitution … so be it.

It is the US Constitution that is the master and not the inbred local socialists in government. If we resist in very physical ways, we would simply be fighting against government terrorism who appear to be determined to steal from us our American way of life and our lands with the threat of financial ruin, prison and land theft.

II. The Rest of the World

In this section, we will take a look at some of the rest of the world and how the NWO is impacting them directly. Some of the dreams presented here indicate what is happening behind the scenes in the spiritual realm. If we can understand what is happening in the spiritual realm, then the mist of confusion lifts from the natural realm and we can see why things are as they are in this world.

In general terms, the Middle East and the lands of the Holy Roman Empire are addressed in this section. The lands under the jurisdiction of the Holy Roman Empire include England, Germany, Switzerland, France, Portugal, Spain and Italy. The Middle East includes all countries that have fallen under the rule of the Islamic jihad.

The spread of Islam has since its very inception been spread by war and fear. It should be understood that the nature of the root will always bring forth its nature in its fruit. There is no such thing as a tolerant Islamic doctrine. To claim such a doctrine is heretical to the writings of Mohammad and a lie spread in the West to make the West open their doors to Islam under false pretenses. In time, Islam will rise up and seek to destroy the European way of life and kill all who oppose their rule.

However, as you will read in the following dreams, there is a unity that will emerge between the Jew, the Christian and the Muslim as they gather together as one army to fight a common enemy as the armies of the Beast. The Beast will come out of the Roman Church in alliance with the Illuminati and NWO. This will be an amazing event of history considering the long standing hatred between these three religions. Who will be raised up to lead them as one army against the Beast?

Chapter 12: Dream - 1000 Caliphates
The dream

In the early morning of the 21st of march , I received a series of three short dream scenes located in different parts of the universe. In all three dreams, there was an angel giving a command from the heavens for certain things to occur.

In the first scene, the Angel spoke to the 'Mooners' who were those who now live on the moon. The Angel said, "To the 1500 Mooners who live upon the moon. Prepare for the wars that are coming to earth and become self sufficient and not dependent upon the earth's resources that will soon become lost in war."

In the second scene, I again heard the Angel cry out to the planets in our solar system, "To the thousands living on the planets of Earth's sun, prepare for the wars coming to earth and store up provisions and become completely self-sufficient that you might survive."

In the last scene, I was somewhere in the Middle East. I again saw and heard the Angel cry out and declared, "1000 Caliphates will be raised up in the land of Abraham to war against the armies of the Beast. They will live as Nomads hidden in the mountains and deserts of the land of promise." I then awakened.

As I considered this last dream scene, I found it most interesting that the title Caliphate was used in the dream since this is exclusively used by Muslims for their theocratic empires and the Caliph was the title of the successors following after Mohammad. Wikipedia defines Caliphate as follows:

> A caliphate (from the Arabic خلافة or khilāfa, Turkish: Hilafet) is an Islamic state led by a supreme religious as well as political leader known as a caliph (meaning literally a successor, i.e. a successor to the prophet Muhammad).

> The term caliphate is often applied to successions of Muslim empires that have existed in the Middle East and Southwest Asia. Conceptually the caliphate represents the political unity of the entire community of Muslim faithful (the ummah) ruled by a single caliph.
>
> In theory, the organization of a caliphate should be a constitutional theocracy, (the Constitution being the Constitution of Medina), which means that the head of state, the Caliph, and other officials are representatives of the people and of Islam and must govern according to constitutional and religious law, or Sharia. In its early days, the first caliphate resembled elements of direct democracy (see shura) and an elective monarchy.

This use of the term Caliphate by the Angel of YHWH seems to suggest at least some Muslims living in the lands promised to Abraham will give their support the rise of 1000 Caliphates who are raised up by YHWH. This would be monumental in these modern times considering the current wars in the Middle East. It would be a coalition that could NOT be anticipated considering the great hatred of Muslims against Jews and Christians.

Muslim - Jewish - Christian Alliance

Only two times in history has this kind of alliance occurred and that was when there was a common enemy that threatened both religions where neither of the armies could overcome a superior force alone. It suggests the armies of the Beast will seek to overcome Islam, Judaism and Christianity as the "people of the book." This alliance is set for sometime in the future were these three religions will put aside their swords against each other and join together in an alliance for a short time to combat against the armies of the Beast.

According to the Holy Scriptures, the armies of the Beast will come down from the North into the Holy Lands to destroy all who oppose him. They will most likely land at Acre on the Coast of Lebanon and then go south toward Jerusalem. What does seem to be open to question is who these 1000 Caliphs will be? Of what sect of Islamic religion and of what race will they descend? Will it be a mixed group representing all of the three one-God religions?

I can say it will not be leadership under the umbrella of the Roman Church or its Protestant children denominations who will side with the Beast by this juncture. It will not be the Holy Roman Empire, the NWO, the Illuminati, the American military or its allies. These nations and people will be among the armies of the Beast with American becoming the two-horned Beast of Revelation who causes the rest of the world to worship the Beast .

The true Christian people of this alliance will be of the Hebrew Church that has been reestablished in Jerusalem by this time. The Jewish people will be Messianic believers in accepting the Messiah Y'Shua as their deliverer. The Muslim people will be those who have seen the coming of Y'Shua as foretold in the Koran as the one who will lead the world back to the one God.

> "Thereupon she pointed to him. They said, 'How can we talk to one who is a child in the cradle?' Jesus said, 'I am a servant of ALLAH. HE has given me the Book, and has made me a Prophet; 'And HE has made me blessed wheresoever I may be, and has enjoined upon me Prayer and almsgiving so long as I live; 'And HE has made me dutiful towards my mother, and has not made me arrogant and graceless; 'And peace was on me the day I was born, and peace will be on me the day I shall die, and the day I shall be raised up to life again.' That was Jesus, son of Mary. This is a statement of the truth concerning which they entertain doubt." — Qur'an, Surah 19:30-35

Covenant of Omar

In such a timely alliance, we may see some version of the Covenant of Omar revisited as the historic foundation to enable such an alliance to occur.

The Covenant of Omar

In the Name of Allah, the Most Merciful, the Most Compassionate. This is an assurance of peace and protection given by the servant of Allah Omar, Commander of the Believers to the people of Ilia' (Jerusalem). He gave them an assurance of protection for their lives, property, church and crosses as well as the sick and healthy and all its religious community.

Their churches shall not be occupied, demolished nor taken away wholly or in part. None of their crosses nor property shall be seized. They shall not be coerced in their religion nor shall any of them be injured. None of the Jews shall reside with them in Ilia'.

The people of Ilia shall pay Jizia tax [head tax on free non-Muslims living under Muslim rule] as inhabitants of cities do. They shall evict all Romans and thieves.

He whoever gets out shall be guaranteed safety for his life and property until he reach his safe haven. He whoever stays shall be [also] safe, in which case he shall pay as much tax as the people of Ilia' do. Should any of the people of Ilia wish to move together with his property along with the Romans and to clear out of their churches and crosses, they shall be safe for their lives, churches and crosses, until they have reached then safe haven.

He whoever chooses to stay he may do so and he shall pay as much tax as the people of Ilia' do. He whoever wishes to move along with the Roman, may do so, and whoever wishes to return back home to his kinsfolk, may do so. Nothing shall be taken from them, their crops have been harvested.

To the contents of this convent here are given the Covenant of Allah, the guarantees of His Messenger, the Caliphs and the Believers, provided they [the people of Ilia'] pay their due Jizia tax.

Witnesses hereto are:

Khalid Ibn al-Waleed Amr Ibn al-Ass Abdul-Rahman Ibn'Auf Mu'awiya Ibn abi-Sifian Made and executed in the year 15 AH.

Great Disjunction

The only other time in history where there was a reported alliance of Muslims, Christians and Jews was during the 3rd Crusade at Acre in which Saladin and King Richard joined forces together against a 3rd/4th dimensional army of Nephilim and demons and other creatures of death. It was called the Great Disjunction. I provided this story in Book 1 but will include it here as well in brief.

In the year 1192, Richard the Lion heart, King of England, ventured across Europe during the Third Crusade. At the height of this aggression the fabric of reality was briefly torn, allowing a short but devastating influx of magic and spirit-kind to be unleashed across the Earth.

When Saladin's forces failed to pay tribute demanded by the crusaders, Richard's trusted adviser whispered to his king that the Muslims should be punished and their threat ended for all time.

The adviser told Richard to gather several holy artifacts to the city so that a divine ritual could be initiated to bless Richard's forces and curse their foes. Believing his counsel, Richard unknowingly brought several powerful artifacts together -- and these artifacts, relics of creation itself, and of such power, began to undo reality simply through their congregation.

As the material fabric of Earth tore, spirit-kind and magic were unleashed across the world. Hordes of demons and strange beings of power sprung up in the streets of Acre, surrounding Richard's army.

After heavy losses, Richard and Saladin joined forces to wade through the hordes. With incredible valor, the two heroes wounded the adviser, now revealed to be a 'dark' magi of considerable power. The adviser fled, along with a host of the evil creatures, allowing Richard and Saladin to seal the breach.

Although the battle lasted but a few hours, the Disjunction, as it would come to be called, unleashed vast forces across the entire planet, changing history forever.

Realizing that the ritual could never be allowed to occur again, both Richard and Saladin swore to divide the relics and secure them in their respective lands. The Knights Templar agreed to protect relics in the west, while the Order of Saladin secured several relics to the east. These two noble orders would band together over the centuries for a series of 'hidden' crusades against the forces of evil that escaped the Disjunction.

It is the event of the shedding of innocent blood that opens the door to the coming and judgment of the Nephilim and demons. This will become a contingent of the military forces of the Antichrist and Beast. What is giving these Nephilim and demons most of their power today is the mass killing of unborn babies in America and around the world. More deaths occur in American due to Abortion than the rest of the world due to all other killers other than the natural death of old age.

Satanic Power from Killing the Innocent

The judgment of America is now overdue where the Nephilim now have the right to rule over America and bring 'just' judgment against its people for their unconscionable shedding of innocent blood. This is the coming great American Holocaust to occur soon in our modern times. It far outweighs the murder of millions of Jews in Nazi Germany.

It will be the Nephilim who will soon be given the 'right' in the courts of heaven to rule over America in the form of the Illuminati self-acclaimed demigods, their Merovingian descended royal houses with their Jesuit occult priesthood.

Mooners and Others

In addressing the other two dreams of humans who currently live on the moon and earth's other planets in our solar system, this has only been made possible by Alien technologies given to human shadow governments. It is now well documented that UFO flying craft can easily leave earth's gravity and go most anywhere since it creates its own secured and buffered environment where air, warmth, food and other necessities can be provided.

This dream of humans living on our moon and planets is the second dream I have had on this reality. The first dream in 2008 was when I met with three angels over earth and they flew me over each planet in our solar system and told me how many humans were currently living on each planet. They did not say how many aliens were also living on each of our planets with the humans so this is unknown to me. As I remember, I was told by the head angel that 500 people were living on Mars in 2008. I do not know how many are living there now.

Chapter 13: Prophetic Letter to the Empress of the Holy Roman Empire

The future is near as prophecy unfolds.
Offer to you they will part of your former throne.

Of you will they ask only that you friend the pope.
One horn supplanting three of the ten is planned.

The name 'Vicarius Filii Dei' shall he wear.
The number of a man of great destiny it is clear.

Ordained you, did I, to the
Culdee way.
To empower you to resist such a
fate.

A Sunday worship will they
degree.
An assault upon the Sabbath will
begin.

The two horns will become the
voice for the old.
To enforce their mark upon every
soul.

This consenting mark in the mind and in the hand of strength
will come.
A mark that is the symbol of the son/sun.

Yet invisible to see yet clear as day.
A mark so bold that species in far galaxies will see.

A Culdee shall I remain hidden in faith.
To war against this noble foe as it plays.

This crossroad you shall soon face dear Queen.
Only once will this choice be allowed to be.

To walk in the mark of the Sabbath rest.
Or enjoy the fruits of Sunday's best.

Before your throne will I one day come.

To remind you of this letter wrote.

Will I be decreed a heretic threat?
Or embraced as a friend of good intent?

Rome will soon come to bring you home.
No need to attack the Vatican gates by storm.

But is this a home of redeeming grace?
Or the home for a bitter soul that is lost to fate?

Beware of the angels of light that come
Beware of the angels of light that come.
Beware of the angels of light that come.

Chapter 14: What Land is Yours?
Jerusalem Decides Land Ownership

All the land of the earth is the Lords. Some land however has been consecrated to him specifically at some point in history by a holy people whereas others have not. Jerusalem is the center of the earth for worship and priestly intercessions since Melchizedek at the time of Shem, the son of Noah.

The man Melchizedek is a title and not a name that means Michael Zadok which means "high priest who is like YHWH (God))." He was the most high priest-king of Salem and thus also priest over the whole earth. It was for this reason that Abraham gave him the tithe as the real identity of Melchizedek was Shem and he was most certainly the most holy man upon the face off the earth during the time of Abraham.

Holy Lands

In every country, there are places that are 'Holy Unto the Lord' and it is to these places that the remnant will in time migrate for the protection of the angels and the armies of YHWH led by King Y'Shua. As Americans, we can forget Democracy, Constitutional Republics and the like. The government of Y'Shua is a Theocracy and only the holy are listened to in this government as they immerse themselves into the faith of YHWH enabled by the sacrifice of Y'Shua. There is no voting and no mob rule. It is one man-god at the top who is the historic Y'Shua.

You Own Nothing

If in America, the land that you think you own that you call home is not yours. If you are paying taxes. If you are complying with the zoning rules. If you are told how many square feet you must build and that you cannot live in a trailer on your property, you are the servant to another making these decisions for you.

If you are obedient to a neighborhood board then it is theirs (the government) and is not your land. You are just a tenant and it is owned by others with power over you who have given themselves to socialism that expresses itself in the form of fascism or communism.

If you really owned your land, you would not be paying taxes and would not have to get permission to build anything and then have to get permission modify what you have built. The American ideal of ownership is a farce – does not any longer exist.

The car you call 'my car' you do not own either. You pay to get it licensed and then are taxed to have permission to drive on the roads. You are forced to insure the vehicle you drive and the police of these masters of yours will take away what you have and take away your liberty and may throw you in jail if you do not do what they tell you must do.

You own nothing as an American and you are little more than a slave in the current hijacked economy. Even the gold and other valuables you think you own and have saved for more difficult times are now owned by the US government as per Executive Orders that let them take it from you whenever they want and then just give you a 'company voucher' of some buying power of a value that they will determine later. Even if you grow a garden, there is current legislation that will make it illegal without a license to grow your own food in America. You own nothing.

Slaves and Masters

Since we own nothing, why are we spending so much time gathering so many rented things around us to use that we will never own? Are we so confused by the many promises of prosperity that we cannot see beyond the desire for our own comfort?

Smell the winds of change and smell that there are only two kinds of people in the world according to the NWO masters. There is them, the masters, with their police who own everything and there is the rest of the world that are to be their slaves and own nothing.

Some will confess that, "If they come to take away my land, I have a rifle and will protect what is mine." I then think...so you have a small bore hunting rifle and they have an Apache helicopter with 50 cal. machine guns that can shoot so many rounds in a few seconds that there would be no tree standing in your area and your house would instantly become a pile of rubble.

If that fails, they have heat (your body heat) seeking missiles that will leave just a hole in the ground where you once stood. Yes... this is a great sense of hope in defending your own Constitutional rights as an American. Rambo was a riveting movie but being realistic, our survival in his shoes is most unlikely.

It makes me laugh inside when people tell me all this as they trip dysfunctionally over a pile of empty beer cans in some Rocky Mountain saloon with their belly's hanging over the bar. Believe me, I have heard many make this absurd confession.

Learning from History

If we are to learn anything from history, the American Revolution only was able to make progress because Patriots hid most of the time as the British stood out in the open as easy targets. This American approach in warfare was considered cowardly in the day and made many British officers very angry.

The method was taught to the Patriots by the Native Americans. In more modern times, both the might of the USSR/Russian Army and the US/NATO armies have sought to remedy the threat of the mountain fighters in Afghanistan. Neither Russia (former USSR) or America has been able to achieve their objectives in securing the control of the mountains of Afghanistan. Why?

The Afghans rode horses and stayed among the rocky areas that provides protection. These areas have very narrow paths - almost like trenches naturally cut through the rocks that only a horse can get through. There are many such paths as a means of escape after their quick offensive attack. They attack quickly and leave quickly before they can be easily targeted by the big guns and missiles.

We as Americans and NATO have nothing that can effectively follow in pursuit with all of our inventions of war that we have created. Both invading countries have sought to put their military on horses to pursue the enemy but are met with deadly ambush traps.

Wise Leadership

A wise general will choose the area of engagement that gives them the greatest advantage considering the resources available to both sides. The Western front in Afghanistan has spent billions – the Afghans have spent perhaps thousands and they still hold the 'higher' ground. The current approach is to pay off members of the Afghan tribal forces to have them turn on their family and friends. This has proven ineffective since they are tribal and their commitment to each other is in their blood and is a matter of tribal honor.

What We Should Learn

The Christians should learn from this. Since we own nothing in America anyway, we have nothing to loose.

In resisting evil we can loose nothing except the loss of a hectic life of working to gather rented stuff that is owned and controlled by others to make our life a little easier for a short period of time.

The fact is we will continue to have to give up more of our liberties as time progresses to retain use of the rented stuff. At some juncture, every person in America will have to give up their very souls to the NWO and to the Beast to keep use of the rented stuff.

I strongly encourage each of you reading this chapter to find the 'holy lands' close to you where the Lord Jehovah will provide his angelic protections.
How do we know where the holy lands are?

YHWH leaves us a sign to follow. One such sign is the proto-Hebrew Ten Commandments found in Los Lunas, NM, dating between the 8th and 12th century. This sign is a mark on the land saying it is "Holy unto YHWH" and cannot  be claimed by the NWO as theirs.

The NWO will not be able to control all US lands and will seek to quarantine certain 'problematic' areas that they cannot overcome, like in Afghanistan, and then seek to control the rest of the people of America – mostly by herding them into large cities. American forces will join with selected UN forces including massive forces from China, Russia and other countries to assist in the management (they call it 'peace keeping forces') of the enslaved Americans.

I believe this is part of an agreement with China is in exchange for the massive importation debt we owe to them. Who does Walmart really work for as a primary distributor of China made products? There profit becomes the American debt to China? This debt may be used to justify China's acquisition of many of the American natural resources when they come with their armies into America.

What Land is the Lords in America?

We may begin this quest by asking "What land was taken by lies and treachery by the Federalists?" A couple of thoughts on this. Certainly all Native American Reservations are NOT under US law by historic treaty despite what later US governments and US Courts through history would say about this.

Tribal lands are sovereign native territories although as long as Native Americans continue to receive Federalist funds, they will continue to bow to their masters. I might just get up one morning and go join a reservation somewhere. Certainly, there remains an existing covenant of friendship between the Native Americans and the Culdee (Hebrew Celtic Church) dating as far back as the 8th century. This is evident in the Ojibwe prophecies and in the 'quiet' archeological discoveries of the Anasazi civilization dating between the 8th and 12th centuries in the 4-Corners area of America.

Secondly, the Southern States that were held under severe Martial Law just after the Civil War and who were not allowed to return to the liberties of the Constitutional United States until they signed the 16th Amendment are still under international law free States.

This forced signing into law by many of the Southern States of this treacherous 16th Amendment granting States powers to the Federalists was signed under threat and the shadow of the barrel of many Federalist guns.

International law would not consider this to be a just or valid enactment of law since it was dune under duress. However, the Northern States that signed willingly are lost. Sorry about that. The existing US Territories at the time of the enactment of the 16th Amendment may still be open game. Colorado did not become a State until 1875.

If you are a resident in the Northern States, move to the South or go join an Indian Reservation somewhere in America. Look for evidence of the Mark of YHWH on the land such as the Decalogue found in Los Lunas in New Mexico. Find the holy places where the NWO cannot make a claim of ownership and go there to live. Be led by the Holy Spirit in finding these holy places for you, your family and friends. Learn to live solely from the resources of the land living simply and in peace.

III. Preparing for Battle

The section on preparing for battle looks to what is needed by each YHWH Warrior so he or she will be ready for battle to throw off the assault of the enemy. In this we are to discover many safeguards that should become our daily way of life in living as a protected people.

The Holy Scriptures are both the Old Testament and the New Testament. Y'Shua said he did not come to do away with the law but to fulfill the law. In Timothy where it says, "All scripture is given for reproof, instruction and teaching...." it was referring exclusively to the Old testament since the New Testament had not been compiled at this time in history.

The power of your protection as a YHWH Warrior and Knight is in your fervent daily devotion in upholding the 10 Commandments including keeping the 7th day Sabbath, the daily putting on of the Armor of God and, adherence to the principles found in the Tabernacle of David. The Tabernacle of David is to be reestablished in the last days according to the Holy Scriptures and it is a liturgy or way to reconcile us back to YHWH on a daily basis.

Chapter 15: The Sabbath Rest
What Day is the Sabbath?

When is the most holy day of the week? As the Pentateuch states, it is the keeping of the Sabbath that will be the sign to the nations that the Hebrews are the people of YHWH. Rome through their Pope in assuming the title as the 'Vicar of Christ' has changed the day to a Sunday from the original Saturday. This began in the 4th century with Constantine who made himself the head of the Church in presiding over the Council of Nicea.

If the worship on Saturday is the sign of the people of YHWH, what is the primary worship on Sunday the sign for? What it does do is make all churches that worship on Sunday a 'child' of the Roman Church system. Protestants are then the children of Rome despite their rants and ravings to the contrary. As a child of the Roman Church system, you a a Protestant become the child of the "Vicar of Christ" which when translated into Roman numbers adds up to 666 which is the Mark of the Beast. There is an alternative Church – the true Church of Y'Shua.

Church of Jerusalem in Exile

The Culdee (Hebrew-Celtic Church) held services on both Saturday and Sunday as did the New Testament church in Jerusalem. The Culdee churches in Britain are the last remnant of the Church of Jerusalem in exile holding to the original Hebrew faith and practice. They would honor the Sabbath according to their Hebrew teaching and then meet together on the first day of the week to further study the Holy Scriptures and hear the teachings of the Apostles. It was called a 'dual altar' among the Culdee in celebrating the Eucharist (Communion) on both Saturday and Sunday.

In addition to the Sabbath, there are other Holy Days throughout the year that were evident before Moses codified all into the Pentateuch circa the time Israel left Egypt and entered the promised land of Canaan.

Annual Holy Days

There is the 1) Passover, 2) Unleavened Bread, 3) First Fruits, 4) Pentecost, the 5) Feast of Trumpets following by the, 6) Day of Atonement and finally the, 7) Feast of Tabernacles. These are the seven fasts given to Israel and to the Church by YHWH. The early Hebrew Church of Jerusalem celebrated all seven of these feasts each year.

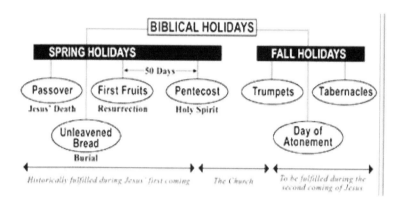

If the Mark of the Beast is the 666 reflected in the exclusive Sunday worship which is the Roman day to worship the Sun also named Mithra and Ra as a god, Saturday is the day of worship of YHWH and the 7th day has not changed since the time of Creation and has been the day of rest upheld by man since the Garden of Eden .

Paganism Intrusion

Further intrusion of paganism by Rome is in celebrating the day of Ishtar (Easter) which is the worship of Isis and fertility thus we find rabbits and eggs as a part of the Roman Easter celebration. This date is different to the Hebrew calender day for the Passover and thus it is a different holy day that is totally of pagan origin.

Our Roman and Protestant Christmas is actually the worship of the rebirth of Mithra that reoccurs every 25th of December on the Roman Calender and was celebrated long before Y'Shua was ever born. One of the activities of the worship of the rebirth of Mithra was the exchange of presents and parties.

It is believed Y'Shua was born in the Spring, Summer or Fall and not in the middle of Winter since the shepherds were in the fields tending their sheep. They would not be in the fields in the winter but tending their sheep in barns, caves or enclosures protected from the cold weather.

The Christmas tree provides for the worship of the spirits of nature who alight upon the tree. This Christmas liturgy is drawn from Druidism and Wicca practices. People would honor or worship nature spirits by saying, "Oh what a beautiful tree and beautiful lights." Mistletoe was commonly used by the Druids to cast a spell over someone.

If you want to be a YHWH Warrior with no chinks in your armor, you must adhere exclusively to only the Holy days of celebration given to us by YHWH and not the holidays given to us by Pagan Rome.

Chapter 16: Dream -Harp and the Wall of Protection
The Dream

Sister Pascha of Emmaus Abbey in NY was in prayer in January of 2012 and had a dream-vision about the importance of the harp. Here is her dream story.

Hi +David,

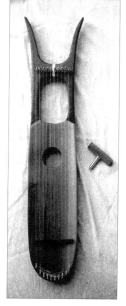

Here is the vision as I saw it while there at the table. It was just a momentary flash but vivid. I saw a large group of people standing all in white and the light around them was a white light very brilliant from each person standing there. They all stood in a group that appeared to be hundreds strong and carried a small version of your harp.

Some in the group were playing a single note while others weren't playing anything but were standing as one. The word I got was that this "wall of sound was protection." Unsure of the single notes being played, I just wondered at this vision.

Pascha

As I consider this dream, it brings back studies that I have conducted in the past on music. In brief, here are some of the findings.

1. When Creator made earth, his spirit hovered over the 'firmament' that was without form and void and and spoke.... no... not spoke but <u>sang</u> the world into existence.
2. The people of Israel in bringing down the walls of Jericho sang with harps and other instruments to cause the walls to fall.
3. All of the Old Testament of the Bible was sang and never just read. It is believed by some scholars that the Word of God' is incomplete unless is has its corresponding melody for each verse. The 8th century Masoretic Torah texts have a character above the Hebrew that is believed to be the original notes that were sung. Based on the work of Haak-Ventura, many of the original melodies have now been transcribed for singing these texts with its original music.
4. Mosley in the 19th century discovered that all of the elements in the periodic table are an octave apart based on ascending atomic weight if you compare the square root of the frequencies that cause each element to gain energy and begin to glow.
5. Keely also in the 19th century was able to cause the molecules of elements to dis-connect themselves and disintegrate into a very fine powder including quartz by just using sound waves. He was also able to cause water to break into hydrogen and oxygen with sound and built a highly efficient engine on this principle. It was determined that music frequencies in the realm of light were the force that holds matter together. He was also able to cause heavy masses to levitate in a jar with music thus changing their mass weight. He was also able to cause mass to disappear into a different (4th?) dimension.
6. The earth has a pulse frequency that is known as the Schumann Resonance that is a composite pulse of near 7.8 cycles per second. This varies somewhat over time but is fairly constant.

7. The Pyramid of Giza has been tested for its internal sound resonance. The tone resonance discovered is near the note of 'A' but is really a multiple of the 7.8 cps of the Schumann Resonance. If 7.8 is multiplied to near 'A' which is the equal temperament pulse at 440 cps, it is 436.8 or 56 times the Schumann resonance of earth. It may be that this is the note that is the fundamental note of earth and of creation on earth in general.

8. The Chinese in history would change their scale keys about every 100 years to coincide with the natural change in the Schumann Resonance and all instruments were tuned to this new fundamental. This assured their music was in harmony with earth and not dissonant with earth. Finding the new frequency fundamental of earth was an intuitive process of finding the chant frequency that caused a peace of the spirit and soul.

9. Sound has been used to create a virtual 'wall' or force that resists entry by matter including humans. Some equate this to a wall of high density static charges but in considering the makeup of static charges, they are just energy in motion sustained or bonded together by sympathetic vibrations or music.

10. The thoughts of the mind and body functions can be controlled by the projection of sound in ultra low frequencies often generated by two microwaves of a few cycles difference that are brought together to create a pulse within the human body that is the difference between the two. Entrainment occurs as this ultra low sound energy bombards the mind at its currently functioning frequency (12-30cps) and then is slowly altered where the mind is captured by this and then follows the beat change. Mood changes and even sleep (6-8 cps) can be made to occur against the will of the human target and can be directed at masses of people for mind-control. Microwave phone towers have this dual frequency mind-control capability.

11. Of all of the instruments, certain instruments that are musically open, uncompressed and free to continue to sound. These are the most effective in bringing peace or relaxation to the hearer. For the strings, it is the harp. For the woodwinds, it is the flute. For the percussion, it is the timpani, bells and chimes and for the brass, it is the native horns made from animal horns.

Song of Creation

It may be this is a message for us to focus on a type of music and sound in utilizing all of the facts provided above. It may be said that singing the Words of Creator are the only words or songs that can alter the state of creation. It does say in scripture that "Creator inhabits the praises of his people." Open sound types of instruments are strongly suggested in this dream-vision. The tuning suggested must be in harmony with nature. Finally, I can say the human voice is perhaps the most effective instrument in impacting a change upon creation. The only thing that remains is in what language should we sing? What was the real Hebrew spoken at the time of Noah?

Davidic TAW Harp

Before we get to the language question, let's consider the shape of the Davidic Harp found on the Hebrew temple coin circa 132 AD. It is the shape of the TAV, TAU or TAW which represents the sound of the letter T or Th.

The original hieroglyph of this symbol was the glyph of a yoke or hobble as the 'U' shape which is the shape of the lyre-harp. It can be spiritually surmised that as we take on the yoke of Creator (YHWH) and sing his praise, we are then in his protection.

The harp is a literal symbol of this protection that has been given to us as the people of YHWH. As time progressed the 'Tav' took on the shape of a cross which is associated with the 'T' with the cross becoming our protection. This occurred long before Messiah Y'Shua was placed on a cross to remedy the debt of sin upon the human race.

The Tav, Taw or Tau literally, this means "mark" or "sign," and it is also a symbol for "vehicle of sacrifice." Tau as the final letter in the Hebrew alphabet and represents completion of the Spiritual Cycle and is a sign of Truth and Perfection. It denotes the final spiritual destination for humankind and is closely associated with the preceding letter shin.

The Hebrew word for "mark" is the letter "X". The Greek translation of the Bible translated it "T". However it its earliest form, it was the shape of the harp held horizontally as indicated by the symbol above. In the book of Revelation, each of the 144,000 prophets were given a harp as a sign of their being 'sealed' in messiah in

being protected from harm during the Great Tribulation. The harp player to the right was found in Egypt and is know to be a Semite or Hebrew.

In Ezekiel 9:4, the prophet Ezekiel has a vision in which God tells a man to mark a "Taw" upon the forehead of those who are to be saved from destruction. The early Christians saw this as a foreshadowing of the Jesus' crucifixion and of the sign of the cross. There are, for instance, first century stone coffins in the catacombs on which the Tau is inscribed."

"And the LORD said to him [one of the four cherubim], 'Go through the city, through Jerusalem, and put a mark [literally, "a tav"] upon the foreheads of the men who sigh and groan over all the abominations that are committed in it.' And to the others he said in my hearing, 'Pass through the city after him, and smite; your eye shall not spare, and you shall show no pity; slay old men outright, young men and maidens, little children and women, but touch no one upon whom is the mark. And begin at my sanctuary.' So they began with the elders who were before the house." (Ezekiel 9:4-6)

Hebrew Today

Modern Hebrew as it is spoken today is not likely the original pronunciation of the Hebrew spoken at the time of creation or even in early Israel at the time of Y'Shua. Modern Hebrew comes from Ashkenazim speakers (Khazars of Esau origin) who spoke with varied Eastern European accents and pronunciations that were very guttural and harsh for some words.

It is my belief based on recent research that certain native languages such as Hawaiian, Ainu, ancient Basque, Dravidian and some Native American languages are actually closer to the pronunciation sounds of the original Hebrew language of creation in that the pronunciation is like the 'peace' instruments - open and unconstrained.

Virtually all of the earliest words of these ancient native languages mentioned end in vowels allowing for sustained open tones in music that is consistent with the nature of peace and peace instruments.

Language Hurdle

Edo Nyland has conducted an extensive study through his life time in seeking to rediscover the original language that existed before the event of the Tower of Babel when it says that "man then become divided due to the many new languages they then began to speak." Prior to this event, it is believed that all mankind had a common language and this language was based upon the language given to them by Creator as also the language of the angels and perhaps even the language of creation itself.

Based on Edo Nyland's research and conclusions, the most ancient languages as traced to the pre-Babel language are constructed of Vowel - Consonant - Vowel (VCV) groupings as the basic building blocks of the original language. Thus the name DAVID may have actually originated from ADA AVI IDE or ABE AVI if the Hebrew form of 'Dawi' is used.

Using the early Basque VCV roots with the connecting vowels doubled for each sub-word, it it translated, ADA/ABA 'the father' AVI 'who is loved' IDE 'by many'. In English from the Hebrew, it is translated as just 'Beloved' that does not paint a complete picture of the meaning of the name David.

Native American Script

Upon initial review, it would appear that the Algonquin language of Natives of North America has a similar VCV structure. This is one of my current areas of research as I dwelt close to the Akwesasne Reserve in upstate NY while writing this original chapter.

It has also been suggested that the early Algonquin connected tribes had a written language that can be traced back to early 'Saharan' hieroglyphic origins as suggested by researchers Covey and Collins.

The earliest history in the Sumerian records dating to earlier than 4000 BC confirm a common language used by all humans as being the case.   In this quest, it is only the rediscovery of the original language that is yet to be determined.

Then we will be able to sing the the songs of Creator in its original Hebrew melodic form of the Bible with its original pronunciation dating perhaps to the Garden of Eden. This will be a wonderful day indeed!

Chapter 17: Tabernacle of David Arises from the Ashes

Tabernacle of David

The scriptures prophesy that in the end times, the Tabernacle of David will be seen among the faithful to lead them back to YHWH (Yahweh, Jehovah) before the return of Messiah Y'Shua (Jesus). What is the Tabernacle of David? How does it differ from the Tabernacle of Moses?

A New Priesthood

There will be a new priesthood for the Tabernacle of David according the Holy Scriptures. The new priesthood is really a return to the most ancient priesthood of the Order of 'Melchizedek' which is really a title not a name.   Melchizedek is a combination of two words that in English are Michael and Zadok. Michael means in Hebrew 'Who is like God' whereas Zadok indicates the line of the 'chosen priesthood' appointed by King David.

So the title actually means, "The chosen priesthood who is like God." Y'Shua is now presiding as the high priest and lord of all the earth as our Melchizedek – "the chosen high priest who is like God.".

This priesthood began with YHWH in the Garden who gave it to Adam and was carried down from father to son to Noah who gave it to Shem. According to the earliest historic records of the Church, Shem was titled the Melchizedek as the son of Noah upon Noah's death.

Shem as the ruling Melchizedek became the priest of the whole earth and passed on this high priesthood to his grandson, Abraham, who passed it down to Isaac and he to the 12 sons of Jacob (Israel) with Ephraim becoming as the firstborn. Moses then took it and gave it to the tribe of Levi and Aaron's sons.

Y'Shua, the Ruling Melchizedek

However, this Melchizedek priesthood was also later given to King David and his sons by a divine act of YHWH and from his line descended Y'Shua who received this mantle as the final and last high priest of the earth and all of creation as indicated in Hebrews 11. He is the last because death could not hold him and he resurrected from the dead, is alive in the flesh and now sits on the right hand of the Father (YHWH) and will come again to the earth to battle against Satan's forces of evil.

This passing down of the Melchizedek priesthood anointing did not always follow the line of the first born but any son of the line could be chosen and anointed by YHWH to become the next Melchizedek high priest of the earth.

The priesthood of Aaron was done away with at the coming of Messiah Y'Shua but the priesthood of Melchizedek remains and will continue to minister though the Millennium with Y'Shua ruling over all of creation from Jerusalem as the High Priest within the Tabernacle (Temple) of David.

Seven Steps – The Liturgy of David

There is the gate of entry and six pieces of furniture in the Tabernacle of Moses and also in the Tabernacle of David. The only change is that the blood sacrifice for sins is finished with Y'Shua becoming the last blood sacrifice upon the cross. With his resurrection from the dead, he still rules as our Melchizedek. This priesthood now serving in the Tabernacle of David is very different to the Aaronic priesthood appointed by Moses. The priestly claim of the modern Jewish Levites is null and void since the Aaronic priesthood was done away with completely with the coming of the final Melchizedek.

The six pieces of furniture include the Altar of sacrifice, the Lavor of washing, the Menorah of the 7-fold Spirit of God (Holy Spirit), the Table of Communion, the Censor of prayers and the Ark of the Covenant. These six pieces of furniture correspond with the events of Acts 2:37-45 which follows:

"And they continued steadfastly in the [2] Apostles doctrine and [3] fellowship, and in the [4] breaking of bread and in [5] prayers. And fear came upon every soul: and many [6] wonders and signs were done by the Apostles. And all that believed were together and had [1] all things common. And sold their possessions and goods, and parted them to all men, as every man had need." Acts 2: 42-45

Communal Living

I lived in Christian Communes from about 1968 to about 1984. Most of the residents were not very ex-hippies but simply took on the Jesus People way of life as converted Jesus hippies. I first lived in Oregon with Zion Lodge that became Shiloh Ranch then moved to what became known as Light House Ranch in Eureka, California then across the Pacific to Hawaii to live with a very large commune of over 1000 people with many residences who were called the Pilgrims.

My dad led these groups and had me in tow since the age of 12 on living among the hippies. What I did see was the best of communal living and the worst of communal living. Many of the leadership were converted Jews so we lived close to the form of Hebrew Christianity I am describing in this book. I look back now and realize we were Hebrew Christians and didn't even know it. Our big gathering was Saturday evening so we kept the biblical Sabbath. We also observed Passover every year and often Pentecost. This life I experienced at a young age reinforced the need for observing what YHWH gave us in the events experienced in the Tabernacle of David, his Sabbath and his Holy Days.

These seven corresponding events are seen in virtually every historic liturgy as well as in the Tabernacle of David. They are found in the form of the pieces of furniture where each piece provides a step of reconciliation bring us closer back to YHWH. Some will call it a liturgy but it cannot be said to be formal in any sense of the meaning of the term 'liturgy'. It is a way for us to walk and be healed each day.

Table of Historic Liturgies

	Nature: Sacraments BC 4000?	Tabernacle: Hebraic BC 2000	Acts 2: Apostolic Church AD 34	Didache: Syrian AD 96?	Post Apostolic: AD 400?	Stowe: Celtic AD 800?	BCP 1928/79: Anglican
1	Earth: Marriage	Gate of Surrender	Gathering for the Needy	Gathering for the Needy	Bringing the Tithe	Collect	Entrance Rite Collect, Bring Elements
2	Fire: Penance	Altar of Faith (blood Sacrifice)	Apostles Doctrine: Teaching about Blood of Jesus	Reading of the Holy Scriptures: Teaching	Reading of the Holy Scriptures: Sermon	Lessons, Lord's Prayer, Sermon	Reading of the Holy Scriptures: Sermon
3	Water: Baptism	Lavor of Fellowship	Fellowship Dinner: Reconciliation	Prayers and Confessions of Reconciliation	Deacons Liturgy: Kiss of Peace. Collect, Prep elements, Sursom Corda	Prefaces, Benediction, Kiss of Peace, Prayers for dead	Nicene Creed, Prayers of People, Confession of Sin, The Peace
4	Tree of Life: Eucharist	Table of Bread and Drink Offering	Breaking of Bread (Communion)	Thanksgiving, Words of Institution	Consecration Prayer, Thanksgiving for Creation, Sanctus, Thanksgiving for Redemption, Words of Institution, Anamnesis, Epiclesis	Joint Prayer of Consecration, Communion Anthems,	Holy Communion: Great thanksgiving, Eucharistic Prayers
5	Wind: Confirmation	Censor of Prayers	Prayers of the Church	Prayers for Deliverance	Lord's Prayer, Great Intercession, Fraction & Elevation, Partaking	Oblations and Offertory	Lord's Prayer, Breaking of Bread, Fraction, Partaking, Absolution
6	Thunder: Orders	Menorah of Revelation	Signs and Miracles	Prophet's Speak, Appeal to God's Power	Reservation of Bread for Sick	Reservation of Elements	Reservation of Elements
7	Rain/Mist: Unction	Ark of Worship	Worship	Thanksgiving	Celebrant's Intercessions	Eulogiae	Post Communion Prayer

89

Chapter 18: Tabernacle   Celebration
7 Stations of the Tabernacle

The seven stations of the Tabernacle of David which the bible says will be revived in the last days provides a means whereby we can be reconciled with YHWH. If we take these steps seriously, we will be renewed and forgiven of our sins and be in fellowship with our creator YHWH. The sequence of steps or stations provide for us a frame for our approach of YHWH as per his plan for us.

1. Gate of Giving

As we come to the Gate of Giving, the books of our heart and life are open to YHWH. We come in humble adoration giving of ourselves and of our increase understanding that it is the Lord that has made provision for us on this earth.

For the Hebrew, the law required a tithe of the tenth of his increase to be given to YHWH by placing it in the care of his ministers. All is the Lord's and we must come to YHWH in his Tabernacle with an open hand and heart.

2. Altar of Forgiving

The Altar of Forgiving was the place were the blood of the sacrifice was shed. It was symbolic of the future coming lamb of YHWH that would die for the sins of the whole world.

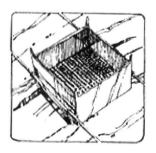

At this station of the Tabernacle, we come to YHWH to receive His forgiveness. In the measure that we are to be forgiven, we must also forgive others. Rabbi Saul told us, "Beware that a root of bitterness not grow up within you for from this many [believers] have been defiled."

3. Lavor of Washing

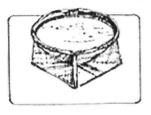

The Lavor of Washing is the third station where we are to fully commit ourselves to YHWH and take on the Name of Y'Shua as our only Messiah. This symbolism is sealed in the act of baptism into the Messiah and into the Word of the Messiah.

Y'Shua said, "It is not the hearers of the word but the doers of the word that are my disciples." The act of baptism is the commitment of discipleship to the Messiah. This mystery was also evident when Y'Shua baptized his own disciples in the form of foot washing just prior to the last supper before his crucifixion.

4. Table of Covenant

The power of the Kingdom of YHWH was not given to any individual but to the People of YHWH. It is to his congregation that we must become committed in membership.

To share of the same loaf and to drink of the same cup at the Table of Covenant is to commit to those with which we share of these same elements. The Messiah showed us that these elements are supernaturally the body that was broken for our weaknesses and blood that was shed for our sins by our Messiah at Calvary.

5. Menorah of Revelation

The Holy Scriptures speak of the 7 eyes of YHWH and the 7 spirits of YHWH that are in the earth to show His glory. The prophet Isaiah tells us that the spirits of YHWH are prophesied concerning the coming Messiah. They are the 1) Spirit of the Lord, 2) the Spirit of Wisdom, 3) the Spirit of Understanding, 4) the Spirit of Counsel, 5) the Spirit of Might, 6) the Spirit of Knowledge and 7) the Spirit of the Fear of the Lord (Isaiah. 11:2).

It is the work of the Holy Spirit that will teach us and reveal to us the heart and mind of YHWH so we might obey him. Once we hear His word, we can then pray with his authority.

6. Censor of Intercessions

Our mission at this station is to intercede for the people of Israel and for the gentiles that are to come to the knowledge of Y'Shua the Messiah. To bring in the Kingdom of YHWH is to bring down the strongholds of evil and to raise up the banner of righteousness in its place.

Since we have waited upon YHWH for the revelation of His will, it is understood that the prayers that follow will be answered since the request is clearly within the will of YHWH. Angels act on our behalf in bringing about the answer and do fight against the fallen angels in the battle for the souls of mankind.

7. Ark of His Presence

At this station, we have come to the Ark having a giving heart and have forgiven all that have offended us. We have been washed in the waters of baptism, sat at the table of covenant and listened at the menorah of revelation. We have then prayed at the sensor of intercessions with the release of God's Power. Now we are clean to enter the Holy of Holies to be in HIS presence.

It is here that we can have true heart communion and friendship with our YHWH. Here, we can freely worship him and are raised up into the heavenlies to view earth from where YHWH sits as a joint heir with the Messiah in His Kingdom. In this we can now rejoice in that our lives have been fully reconciled to YHWH and he again may provide protection and be our guide through his Holy Spirit.

Layout of the Tabernacle

The layout of the furniture of the Tabernacle of David is according to the following plan given to Moses by YHWH. You will notice it forms the cross with the Gate, Altar and Lavor outside (not shown) lining up with the Censor and the Ark inside the Tabernacle covering. The cross pieces are the Table and the Menorah. This again is the expression of the Hebrew letter Tau representing 'Salvation' that has come with faith in Messiah Y'Shua.

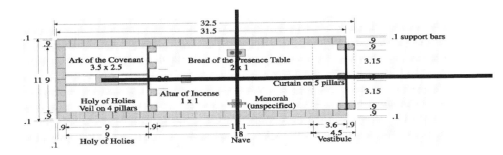

Chapter 19: Armor of God in the Tabernacle

Overcomers

The Armor of God is described in Galatians 6 as needed to overcome the forces of evil. These forces in the demonic realm include Principalities, Powers and the Rulers of Darkness in high places. The six pieces of armor needed to battle evil include the Helmet of Salvation, the Belt of Truth, the Breastplate of Righteousness, the Shoes of the Preparation of the Gospel of Peace and the hand weapons of the Shield of Faith and the Sword of the Spirit.

In Addition, there is a cloak or vestment that covers the body upon which the armor is placed. In the Chapter above, it describes the meaning of the 7 pieces of furniture of the Tabernacle of Moses including the Gate of entry.

What may not be known is the 7 pieces of armor and the 7 pieces of furniture are directly interconnected in spiritual significance. The fact is the Tabernacle as a path to reconcile us to YHWH also places upon us the Armor of God to be able to fight spiritual battles against the armies of Satan. It then follows that the daily ' putting on of the Armor of God' can be effectively accomplished with a morning participation in a form of the Tabernacle liturgy.

Cloak of Covering and the Gate of Giving

`The cloak covers our humanity or sense of self-destiny with the divine destiny of our mission given to us by Creator.

When we enter the Gate of Giving in the Tabernacle, we are putting on the cloak in giving ourselves and our substance to God. We are giving ourselves to God in body soul and spirit as the first step toward becoming one with Creator. We can confess this with the following prayer:

Prayer 1: *I put on the Cloak of obedience and give my life, my strength, my substance and my mind to you Lord God YaHuVeh (YHWH). Lord have mercy upon me*

Helmet of Salvation and the Altar of Forgiveness

The Helmet of Salvation covers and protects the mind where guilt makes its home. At the Altar, we accept the sacrifice of Y'Shua as covering our sins and removing all guilt that plagues our mind. This salvation is made possible by the blood sacrifice of Messiah Y'Shua in removing the curse of sin and guilt. We cannot just think good thoughts and make guilt go away. It must be dealt with by a blood sacrifice that was given to us by Y'Shua at the cross.

Prayer 2: *I put on the Helmet of Salvation and accept the cleansing of the blood of Y'Shua to remove the curse of guilt from my mind. Lord have mercy upon me.*

Belt of Truth and the Laver of the Washing of the Word

The Belt of Truth is our embracing of the truth as delivered to mankind in the Holy Scriptures and by prophecy. It is this truth the keeps us from many deceptions. It is the daily "washing of the water of the word" as represented by the Laver as the scriptures call it where we daily give (wash) ourselves into the teachings of Y'Shua. This includes Baptism in dying to a life of sin by embracing the liberating words of Messiah.

Prayer 3: *I put on the Belt of Truth in the washing of the word of YaHuVeh that I may not fall into the deceptions of Satan. Lord have mercy upon me.*

Breastplate of Righteousness and the Table of Covenant

The Breastplate of Righteousness is your testimony of right living in how you deal with others. The Table of Covenant is where we make covenant with God and with man in the sharing of the common cup and loaf of bread. The communion or Eucharist brings the Church together into one voice and mission in taking within our body collective the saving blood and body of Messiah.

Prayer: *I put on the Breastplate of Righteousness and commit my heart and actions to deal justly and with love with all mankind in covenant with members of the one Church of Y'Shua. Lord have mercy upon me.*

Shoes of Peace and the Menorah of Revelation

The Shoes of the Preparation of the Gospel of Peace is the commitment to in mercy serve the needs of others rather than our own needs. The Menorah represents the mission of the 7 Spirits of God where the Kingdom of God in now established among us and within us on earth.

So far we have made a commitment of obedience to YHWH with the Cloak, then accepted the forgiveness from sin in the Helmet and the Altar and the daily washing of the word of God in the Belt of truth. We further have made a commitment to the true Church of Y'Shua and the world at the Table to deal justly with all others. Now we can reach out to others in bringing peace to them in the form of unwarranted mercy.

Prayer: *I put on the Shoes of Peace that I may reach out to the needy in this world as I receive the guidance of the Holy Spirit in letting the peaceful Gospel of YaHuVeh go out into all the world. Lord have mercy upon me.*

Shield of Faith and the Censor of Prayer

The Shield of Faith is an offensive weapon as well as defensive. Our battle is against the spiritual forces of evil that are in the world under the command of Satan. Our prayers that go up to heaven day and night symbolized by incense from the Tabernacle censor creates this shield for us. Even as incense rises, so should the confession of our mouth in prayers be heard day and night in proclaiming the supremacy of YHWH in the Kingdom of God.

Prayer: *I take up the Shield of Faith to quench all of the fiery darts of the enemy as I pray unceasingly in proclaiming the battle cry of the Kingdom of YaHuVeh. Lord have mercy upon me.*

Sword of the Spirit and the Ark of His Presense

The Sword of the Spirit is that which divides between soul and spirit and good and evil. The Ark of the Covenant is the presence of Creator on earth. It is Messiah Y'Shua who is now the Ark and we the Church who are now the vessels for holding his real presence.

"God is an all consuming fire in which no man can enter and live." "We no longer live but it is Christ who lives within us." As we enter into his rest, he indwells us more fully where just our presence divides good from evil as demons flee in terror.

Prayer: *I take up the Sword of the Spirit that divides between soul and spirit and between good and evil. May I decrease that you YaHuVeh may increase in your unfathomable power in my life. Lord have mercy upon me.*

`As we now have seen, the putting on of the Armor of God does mirror the 7 steps or stations of the Tabernacle of David. This process is a liturgy of preparation for battle against the evil that is in this world. If we do this daily early in the morning, we are preparing ourselves for the day that is to come to bring to earth the supremacy of the Kingdom of Heaven and the divine rule of YHWH and his son, Y'Shua. As we raise up this banner of right living before the world, the world will in due time come to bow before the lamb of God and the power of the cross.

Chapter 20: Breaking the Bonds of Demons and Fallen Angels

The bible says our battle is not against flesh and blood but against evil spiritual forces. Here is the text.

> **"For we wrestle not against flesh and blood, but against principalities, against powers, against the rulers of the darkness of the world, against spiritual wickedness in high places." Ephesians 6:12**

I will keep the hierarchy of evil spirits for another study but do want to focus here on the issue of unknowingly being under the influence evil spirits. There is a difference between a demon and a fallen angel. Demons are disembodied spirits that were once alive as the offspring of the fallen angels and the daughters of men called the Nephilim.

As these Nephilim died, their spirit-souls became demons who now wander through the earth seeking to find another 'body' to indwell to express their evil nature. Fallen angels are of a higher status as heavenly beings but in their fallen state seek to attach themselves to a human soul to cause them to do their bidding.

Seven Curses and Seven Armors

There are 7 ways these demons and fallen angels are given access to attach themselves to a human soul or body. These bondages are presented in this study as curses and they correspond with what the 7 pieces of the Armor of God is to be protecting in avoiding 'alien' intrusion.

> **"Wherefore take unto you the whole armor of God, that ye may be able to withstand in the evil day, and having done all to stand. Stand therefore having your loins girt about with truth, and having on the breastplate of righteousness; And your feet shod with the preparation of the gospel of peace;**

Above all, taking the shield of faith, wherewith ye shall be able quench all the fiery darts of the wicked. And take the helmet of salvation, and the sword of the Spirit, which is the word of God." Ephesians 6:13-17

I will suggest in this study that the 7 pieces of the armor of God are actually intended as 7 prayers that are prayed as symbolized by the pieces of armor. These prayers I provided in the chapter above. It is understood that Faith, hope and love must be the motivation in these prayers as we forgive others in order to be forgiven by YHWH. The description following the armor of God calls us to prayer and is the cloak of supplication.

"Praying always with all prayer and supplication in the Spirit, and watching hereunto with all perseverance and supplication for all saints." Ephesians 6:18

The following chart seeks to bring these principles together showing the curse, how the curse occurs, the armor and a related prayer that will bring deliverance from a bondage to demons and fallen angels.

Curses	Prayers
Family Curses: Inherited from parents or relatives going back many generations. "Cloak of Supplication"	I plead the blood between myself and any evil curse or bondage of my ancestors.
Control Curses: Your thinking is controlled by others. "Helmet of Salvation"	I plead the blood between myself and the forceful will of others.
Word Curses Evil words spoken by you or by others against you or by you to others. "Sword of the Spirit"	I plead the blood between myself and all evil words of destruction.

Trauma Curses Overwhelming memories of pain or a traumatic event. "Breastplate of Righteousness"	I plead the blood between myself and all memories of pain and trauma.
Morality Curses Actions of moral disobedience. "Belt of Truth"	I plead the blood between myself and the curse of all moral sins of bondage.
Ethics Curses Actions of ethical disobedience. "Shield of Faith"	I plead the blood between myself and the curse of unfulfilled promises.
Nature Curses Abuses against nature. "Shoes of Gospel Peace"	I plead the blood between myself and all curses of nature.

The 7 Curses

For each of the 7 curses, praying the 7 prayers will work toward delivering us from these curses and result in our ability to more easily follow the leading of the Holy Spirit and be obedient to the truth of the Holy Scriptures. It is recommended that you pray the prayers daily or anytime you feel under assault by bad thoughts, circumstances or physical illness.

The various curses do not correspond directly to specific physical, intellectual or emotional problems although some observers may begin to recognize certain patterns of bondage related to specific sins. This means that if you are having pain in your body, it could just as easily be the result of a Control Curse as it is a Nature Curse that has come upon you for eating too much junk food.

However the scriptures are clear that we "overcome the devil by the blood of the lamb and the word of our testimony." It is the shed blood of Y'Shua that is painted upon the door posts of our lives that breaks the bonds of the curses. It says in the bible that "Satan comes to maim, kill and destroy" and we need to understand his tactics.

In an earlier chapter in book 1, I presented the dream of the Devils chord that reveals the process of spiritual bondage. It begins with a festering fear that turns into anger. Left unchecked, anger gives way to hate and hate gives place to the spirit of murder - the sin of Cain.

Only the true repentance of the heart can prevent this course of bondage from ultimately destroying a person. We overcome Satan through the forgiving blood of the Lamb coupled with the pursuit of a testimony of obedience.

Family Curses

Family or generational curses are passed on in the womb or sometimes in early childhood. In many families, you may find a common kind of sin that is prevalent in the family. These sins are passed on by demons that attach themselves to families and bloodlines and work to bring all family members under their control. Often witchcraft or satanic worship is involved in the lives of ancestors somewhere in the past to give more power to these curses.

The way to discover if this type of curse in in your life is to conduct a review of the members of your family extended family and see if there are certain kinds of sins that seem to be more prevalent than others. These curses can be resisted and the blood of the lamb placed between you and the demons who once ruled your ancestors. You may pray the form of prayer as follows:

"I plead the blood of Y'Shua between myself and any evil curse or bondage of my ancestors."

Control Curses

Control curses come by the influence of people in your life that have used fear or threat to cause you to become subordinate to their thinking and control.

You can discover this by remembering when you are around certain people, you find you cannot disagree with them and tend to be submissive to their ideals and thinking even if you disagree with them. In fact you find you are afraid to disagree with them.

Sometimes people overcome this with anger in confronting them but this is just the next step after fear leading toward destruction. Breaking their hold over you is done without anger but your peace of mind and heart.

The simple definition of witchcraft is "one person controlling another." To control people does not require incantations to get them but simply playing upon our human fears enables others to get a hold of our minds and thus our life values. Once you discover who these people are by letting the Holy Spirit bring their faces into your mind, you can pray the following prayer for release from their bondage. I would name them by name in this prayer.

"I plead the blood of Y'Shua between myself and the forceful will of others."

Praying this prayer may have to done many times since your mind has to be retrained to think differently. It is also important to know the truths of the bible and start confessing these positive truths to overcome the wrongful beliefs you once held about yourself that made you vulnerable

Word Curses
If someone speaks words to you as in swearing or derogatory language that causes you feel exploited, verbally raped, demoralized, these are curses that are carried in words. We can also say such words to ourselves that causes the same condition of despair. In addition, a curse of words may come by words that we read or even word pictures that we observe. TV is a full of cursings in words that we hear and word pictures portrayed in shows and advertising.

When we close our eyes, what do we see? Can we remember events when someone said things to us that caused us to despair or feel less than human? Horoscopes are often the source of word curses in telling us our futures as inspired by demons.

As we can remember specific events in our lives where we heard words spoken to us like, "you will never amount to anything" or "I wish I were dead" you are under the curse of these words. Repent of embracing them and pray the following prayer.

"I plead the blood of Y'Shua between myself and all evil words of destruction."

Trauma Curses

Trauma curses result from an event that we experienced that caused great distress to our bodies or souls. A tragic death of a loved one, divorce, an accident or rape can all cause a trauma that can give place to a demon to attach themselves to us.

Sometimes traumas cause memory loss because we cannot confront the trauma in our conscience memory. As the outer layers of our many traumas in life are dealt with by the Holy Spirit, often these suppressed memories begin to come back. It is then we can deal with them.

One way to discover if you have a trauma curse is to remember back to all the difficult times you endured and sense if there is still a deep pain in the memory that has not been healed by the tender love of Y'Shua. Forgiveness in this case needs to be extended to those you hold as responsible for the trauma event.

The forgiveness may not be deserving for them but this is for you more than it is for them. It is the path you must walk to be free from bondage. Once repentance has been extended, you may pray the following.

"I plead the blood of Y'Shua between myself and all memories of pain and trauma."

Morality Curses

Morality sin curses often cover the area of illicit sexual relations as either fornication or adultery. It may also include a violation of any of the 10 commandments which are really a moral code for the faithful. Most will agree that stealing, killing, adultery, lying, coveting, are moral sins but also in the list are the sins of idolatry, swearing in the name of God, dishonoring God, dishonoring parents and not keeping the Sabbath are also moral sins. Exodus 20.

Generally if you have done any of these, you are under a morality curse and need to repent specifically for each of these sins. You may followup with the following prayer.

"I plead the blood of Y'Shua between myself and the curse of all moral sins of bondage."

Ethics Curses

The ethics area of bondage normally rests with our commitments and promises and whether we fulfill these commitments and promises to others. This could be in the context of business, family, society or anywhere we have made a commitment to do something and then have not fulfilled our promise.

In many cases, it is possible to think back and remember the commitments we have made in business or family and then ask ourselves, "Did I not fulfill them?" If not, you need to go and as much as it is possible remedy these commitments. Certainly restitution is necessary if it is possible in seeking their forgiveness.

The bible says to "leave your gift at the altar and then go a be reconciled with your brother and then return and offer your gift to God." This means that a large part of the liberation from the bondage of this curse is in doing restitution. Once restitution and forgiveness is completed, you may pray the following prayer.

"I plead the blood of Y'Shua between myself and the curse of unfulfilled promises."

Nature Curses

The final type of curse comes from a sin against nature itself. There is some support that all moral sins are also sins against nature since at the creation, these truths were integrated into the very fabric of nature. I agree with this view.

When we murder, we sin against the Creator who created man. We sin against ourselves in taking innocent blood and we sin against nature as the blood goes into the earth and finds no place of peace in the soil. God heard the blood of Abel as it cried out from the earth after being murdered by Cain.

Sins against nature also relate to the task of being the watchman or husbandman over the earth as good stewards of the earth. This task was given to Adam and to all his seed. Any act then that causes the earth to be destroyed such a pollution and the decimation of forests without replanting is a sin against nature and comes with a curse.

In Revelation it says in the last days the earth shall rise up against those that have done treacherously against her. If we have left a 'nature place' better than we found it, we are to be blessed. If we leave a 'nature place' less productive than when we found it, we are under the curse of nature. Once repenting and seeking to remedy the sin by replanting or cleaning, we can then pray the following prayer

"I plead the blood of Y'Shua between myself and all curses of nature."

Conclusion

We have covered the 7 curses and the 7 armors of God that are 7 prayers of deliverance to free us from curses that may be upon our life. Every one is under a curse in some area of their life. To say you are not under a curse is to say you have no sin and the bible says that such a person is a lair. If you lie, you are just adding more curses to your life.

Freedom should be the cry of every heart. If you give time for the Holy Spirit to take you through the Armor of God associated with the prayers of deliverance, you will become liberated to such an extent that you will become a different person living in the character of Y'Shua our Messiah.

Chapter 21: Abbot Delivered From Satan
Bitterness Destroys

Now this is where it gets personal for me. It may seen strange that a Christian may have a chink in his or her armor that allows certain demons and spirits to use them when certain conditions are just right. Certainly the root of bitterness enables all kinds of spirits to jut walk right in and do their work in the life of a confessing Christian.

If the bitterness in the life of a Christian is not dealt with, in due time, the forces of evil will uproot all that is of faith and the person will be bound with fear and unknowingly begin to do Satan's bidding. Many such people think they are doing the work of the Holy Spirit but they are really doing the work of Satan in dividing the Church, exalting themselves and wounding the saints.

Deliverance Did Not Deliver

I my case, I went through a series of deliverance's in the late 70's led by people who themselves were heavily controlled by fear as enabled by their many harbored bitterness's. As a result, I did not get delivered but actually was given a spirit that attached itself to me and would from time to time give me revelations that were true but not right for the time and not of YHWH.

Divination

I have since learned the nature of this spirit and some of the spirits that used this 'medium' spirit to give me revelations.

It was common in some circles who conducted deliverance to command the demons to speak the truth in Jesus name assuming the demons knew the real truth and that using Jesus name would force them to comply as good honest demons contrary to their natures.

The words spoken were then recorded and became core to their developing theology. The fact is this was a form of divination where demons were consulted about many subjects under the guise of deliverance. This I needed to be delivered from.

Exultation of Self or Humility

Needless to say, I am now going through all of the revelations from God that I have received over the years that I considered mile stones in my Christian walk and now laying them before YHWH and asking for his confirmation of these revelations to determine if they are of him or of Satan.

One way I am being able to determine if they are of YHWH is the fruit. Did they cause division or unity in the Body of Christ? Did they exalt me into grandiose images of self or did they bring me into a more humble state of thinking with regard to self and ministry.

Did these revelations result in people getting saved or just becoming members of a movement or denomination that carried the dog-tag of Christian but was just a shell of faith with no personal relationship to Creator and his son Jesus?

Using these measures, many of the mile stone revelations I have had to throw out and only embrace those that bring spiritual life to me and those I influence.

Confronted by the Empress

It was the Empress of the Holy Roman Empire that brought this chink in my spiritual armor to my attention. As a bishop, I ordained her a Deaconess in 2004 in Hawaii and she has taught me much over the years.

I sure did try to argue out of the facts but in the end, I had to consent that there was something amiss in my Christian armor and walk. I was her personal chaplain and was supposed to be her spiritual guide but she has guided me in persisting in sharing this insight into my need for deliverance.

Most deliverance occurs when we see the truth and close the doors to Satan's access to our minds. In some cases, the demon or spirit has to be addressed directly and commanded to leave. Jesus was very active in this form of ministry and deliverance occurred as much as healing in his ministry.

Modern society is not any less inundated by demons than were the people of the 1st century but we have allowed our science to hide the fact of demons and fallen spirits that still roam the earth seeking a human to inhabit.

Open Confession

Some may think that this open confession may be a detriment and undermine my role as Bishop and Abbot General of the Culdee but open confession is one of the major ways to combat Satan and uproot his work in our lives. Open confession with all of the Church attending was the standard in the early Church and over time, the 'catholic confessional' was created to preserve the honor of those confessing. There might be a better way. If honor is always protected, when then can the events of humility be brought into the life of a growing Christian?

In the 70's while still in my teens, I was a minister in the *Fellowship of Christian Pilgrims* in Kona, Hawaii with the ministry led by Ken Smith, now also bishop and who is my father. At the time, the ministry was under the patronage of Bishop Hanchette of the Episcopal Church of Hawaii before Presiding Bishop Browning was elected and led the American Episcopal Church (ECUSA) into severe heresy.

In this ministry, open confession of sin was a common way to bring about a speedy deliverance and much support was provided by the community to assure a new way of thinking in the mind of the delivered in closing the doors to Satan's way of thought and life.

In the Celtic polity, each abbot and bishop has an Anamchara or confessor that he confesses to to enable counsel and prayer for deliverance. However, this confession is also commonly shared among those that are closest to the Abbot or Bishop so collective prayer may be offered on his behalf.

Two or More

"Where two or three are gathered, there am I in the midst of them" the scriptures tell us. It also says that before two or three witnesses is anything confirmed.

It is wise to include more than one to whom you confess so that the prayers of the Church may be effective and deliverance may be assured.

If openly confessed in the body of Christ, it also enables the 9 spiritual gifts to operate as defined in I Cor 12 so all areas of bitterness and deception may be uncovered and deliverance may be complete. Particularly important to the ministry of deliverance are the gifts of prophecy, knowledge, wisdom and discerning of spirits.

Do You Need Deliverance?

If you sense a need for greater freedom in your life, seek to find a body to confess to so as to enable the ministry of deliverance to occur in your life. It does not matter what position you hold as confession tends to bring people together in trust and support rather than rejection.

If you are rejected by a group you confess to, I would suggest they are like the group that tried to deliver me in the 70's. They have so much buried bitterness, they have become spiritually shipwrecked and are no longer of the Christian faith although they may say all of the right words. It is by the fruit that you will know them and not their words or grandiose titles or even social humanitarian achievements.

The fruit will result in Church unity, humility and a committed support for each member including you. This I can promise you you seek the way of humility and confess your sins to the Church.

Chapter 22: Messiah Jesus ... I mean Y'Shua... I mean...

What's in a Name?

It says that every knee shall bow to the name of Jesus. Was it the name 'Jesus' or was it the name, Yeshua, Yahshua, Joshua, Jahhua or Y'Shua that every knee will bow to? Mmmm... I wonder if it really makes any difference? If you are following Hellenist Christianity, it makes sense to use the name 'Jesus' as this is the Greek-Latin adaptation of the name but if you are following the polity of Hebrew Christianity, then Y'Shua seems more appropriate.

The New Age and now the NWO guys have new names for Jesus like Sananda that are really very different persons to the Y'Shua that died on the Cross and rose from the dead for us.

In this case, it really does matter what name you use. Unless the name solely represents the Jesus or Y'Shua that rose from the dead after a death upon the cross, it is not the Son of God that is being invoked. It is some other imposter spirit with an antichrist 'I want to be god' complex.

In the ministry of deliverance over the last 40 years, we used the name 'Jesus' to expel demons and they know full well who we were naming to require that they leave and they left. They never debated the name of Jesus so translating the name Y'Shua to Jesus does not seem to matter with them. They were not confused by this action in the least. They did debate about whether we had the power through faith in the blood of Jesus to make them go.

A brother studied in Hebrew Christianity confronted me on the question of why I am using the name Jesus rather than Y'Shua? I really had no good reason for this choice other than it is the name more commonly used by the western Churches for our Messiah.

After thinking about this for a few days and doing a study on the name, I have concluded that either name can be used but the actual name that was used by the people of the bible, the Hebrew people and perhaps even by YHWH and the angels in heaven is 'Y'Shua'. Who am I to translate his name from Y'Shua to Jesus just because the Roman Catholic Church tells me I should do this?

So here I am after painting, **"KING JESUS IS COMING!"** on the school bus and now I wonder if I should change it to, **"KING Y'SHUA IS COMING!"** The length of the words Jesus and Y'Shua are about the same so it would fit into the space.

In pursuit of the original Hebrew Christianity, it is only fitting to use the original Hebrew name of our Messiah which is Y'Shua. Some use the extended form of Jahshua or YahShua which really is the English name Joshua. I shall remain with Y'Shua and call upon him for faith to be an overcomer.

Well... I did change the name on the school bus from Jesus to Y'Shua. I feel much better about it all now that I am using Y'Shua.

VI. Nature and Technologies

Most of the occult world is in the search of power to rule over others to ultimately gain wealth, comforts and honor so they may live as gods on earth. In many cases, the 'powers' used by the occult practitioners are powers found in nature but have over the thousands of years of man's existence become associated with a demon or spirit. These spiritual guides lead them into the use of these powers who in return demands their servitude.

In this section, I am sharing a few dreams that identify some of these nature powers and suggest some technologies that may harness these natural powers. In doing this, I am aware that many who have a lust for power will miss completely the purpose of my sharing this information on these powers that originally came from YHWH. They will rather choose to use these powers for their own benefit. This is sad.

Having worked for DAARPA in sensor development and instructed in robotics and sensor system development for 5 years at a technical college in Hawaii, I do have a hands-on background in these technologies. I can only hope that good will overcome evil as we approach the soon return of Messiah Y'Shua.

Chapter 23: Dream - Power of the Merkaba
The Dream

The dream was received in the early morning of the 17th of February 2013. For clarity, the Merkaba is a three dimensional star of David made of two three sided pyramids that are intersecting with the alignment of the center of mass for each pyramid in making a three dimensional shape of the Star of David.

Meaning of Merkaba

The CV root terms for Merkaba are Me Re/Ra Ka Ba. These are all terms relating to the power of the Egyptian gods and the spirit-soul of man. These can be easily researched from many existing sources. Even through the Egyptian gods are associated with the Merkaba, the device is not a god in itself. It is simply an energy device used by the lesser 'gods' to achieve power to their rule over the earth and the weaker souls of mankind.

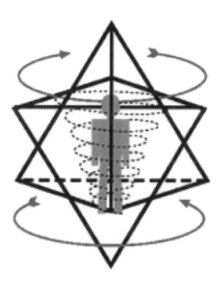

The dream provided a working detail plan of the construction of a crystal power source for usable energy – more specifically electrical energy. It is understood that such energy exists all around us and is called scalar energy an has been use din many zero-energy devices. Zero-energy simply means a device seems to get more energy out of it than is put into it but this is in discounting scalier energy that exists in great density all around us.

Scalar Energy Devices

Tesla and others found a way using special crystals to capture this energy to power cars from a power collector held in a little black box they carried with them and then just plugged this little box into their electric cars to power the electric motors driving the wheels. The power source in the box never needed to be charged. It charged itself and had enough power to drive a car at normal speeds and at unlimited distances.

However, these designs have been hidden by our own shadow government so we continue to remain dependent on fossil fuels for energy and remain dependent upon government to provide these for us.

Now for the dream.

In the beginning of the dream I saw two three sided crystal clear pyramids floating in air and then merge into one merkaba crystal. It appeared to be made of a rock crystalline material that was clear and looked like quartz.

Making of the Crystal

The scene then changed and I then I saw a glass lab beaker about 3 inches across and 4 inches deep with a solution in the beaker that was slightly cloudy white. I immediately understood this in the dream to be Orme or Ormus materials made from precious metals. I then saw a 1" thin band of silver-gold looking polished metal around the outside of the beaker and a wire from the side of the metal band connecting to some machine device.

Suspended from the top of the beaker to the center of the beaker by a micro thin gold wire (could not hardly even see it) was a small gold bead.

I then heard a chord sound come from the machine device that seemed to vibrate the metal band located around the beaker very slightly. There were 4 tones sounding together in making the chord of a 4-note harmonic chord.

As I watched the beaker, the milky white beaker solution began to be attracted to the gold bead in the center of beaker and began to form a merkaba shaped crystal that was clear. The crystal grew larger and larger as I watched until it was about 2″ across in all directions in the shape of the two intersected 3-sided pyramids known as the merkaba.

The Power Device

The beaker then disappeared and I then saw the new merkaba crystal that was just created now suspended in mid air. It looked like the crystal I saw in the beginning but now had the same 1″ wide thin metal band suspended around it and this band was connected to a sound generating device.

On the top of the crystal there was a small gold cap and also had the same gold cap on the bottom of the crystal. Attached to each cap point was a gold-soldered gold wire that went off to the right from the top and bottom of the caps on the crystal. These wires were understood to be the power terminals for accessing the power of the merkaba crystal that generated electricity when the chord was sounding through the resonant metal band around the crystal.

Ancient Djed Device

Still in a dream state, I then saw a very ancient device used by the Egyptians called the Djed.   This was a device thought to be a power device of ancient origin. I understood in the dream that it housed the merkaba crystal and harnessed the power from the crystal that was an electrical beam like power that could be directed.

Near the top of the Egyptian Djed power device were 4 bowls that were like bells that when sounded together created the 4-note chord needed by the crystal to collect scalar energy and then generate extreme electrical power.

The beam of electrical energy was almost laser in form and would then emanate from the crystal through the top end of the device and wield very destructive power against an enemy of those who operated the device. The dream then ended.

Why the Dream?

I do not know why I received this dream. Some years ago I did research into Orme and Ormus materials and how to make them from precious metals. The most common metals used were silver, gold, platinum, rhodium, iridium and others. Any precious or even semiprecious metal could be used resulting in different characteristics of the white powder with varying biological and energy effects.

ORME Characteristics

This material although made form precious metals was affected by magnetics and would jump periodically when in a strong varying magnetic field. The jumping action which I have observed personally seems to be associated with the diatomic cycles of positive and negative magnetic switching occurring within the material.

In addition, ORME materials are known to be a super conductor and once gold or other metals were altered to this diatomic state, it no longer reacted like a metal chemically or electrically. Other experiments have shown that it can change its weight under certain conditions in converting some of its mass into energy that seems to carry over into the 4th dimensional state. It has also been seen to levitate off of a table under certain conditions. In some experiments, it has exploded with such power that its release of power was more nuclear in nature than conventional.

Because each metal had a different effect on life, it suggests each metal resonates with a different set of frequencies in modifying adjacent biological cells. These new materials are currently being tested for the healing of different diseases such as cancer.

Missing Design Details

Specific design information is missing in this dream description of the merkaba power source to make the building of the device unlikely. The needed details include the type of metal(s) used in the Orme solution for making the crystal and the metal(s) used in the band for sound resonance and most importantly the 4 notes that energized the band and later the crystal to capture, transduce and give off usable electrical energy. I remember hearing the 4 tones in the dream but I am not sure I could identify them now.

Chapter 24: Power of the MAGI Cross
Why the Magi Cross?

This chapter is really theoretic more than prophetic or biblical. It is my attempt in seeking to understand the various dimensions in which different created species seem to dwell and function. Not all of God's creation is bound to the $3^{rd}/4^{th}$ dimension where mankind mostly dwells. YHWH himself lives within in the 12th dimension and functions throughout all other dimensions according to my theory presented here.

I have chosen to use what I call the Magi cross (right) for illustrating this theory. This cross predates Christianity by at least 800 years where it was found among the Chinese in referring to the 'shining ones' or those enlightened with the priesthood and wisdom of God himself.

Some of these priests were originally of the Order of Melchizedek and were of Hebrew origin. Others came from the Order of the Serpent and the line of Cain. The Melchizedek Order began with Adam and was passed on to Noah. It was carried forward by Shem the grandfather of Abraham where Abraham carried this order into the Hebrew people through Isaac and then Jacob (Israel) and then to King David and Solomon.

Today this hereditary priesthood remains divided at the time of Shem with some following the way of YHWH while others following the way of Sama-el and the Nephilim.

The Three Wise Men

The three wise men came from the East and knew of the Astrological signs for the coming of the true Messiah. They brought with them gifts suitable for the acknowledgment of a King of Kings and the Messiah for all peoples. Both King and Messiah were found in one person. They were members of this ancient Magi priesthood of the Melchizedek line and were told by YHWH to not return to Herod to tell him that they had found the Messiah but to return home to the East (China?) by another way.

12 Rays of Truth

Within the Magi cross found all over the world, there are 12 lines or rays of power emanating from its simple form. Each of the rays represent 12 truths or realities in 12 subject areas and each of these subjects have 12 subdivisions within them.

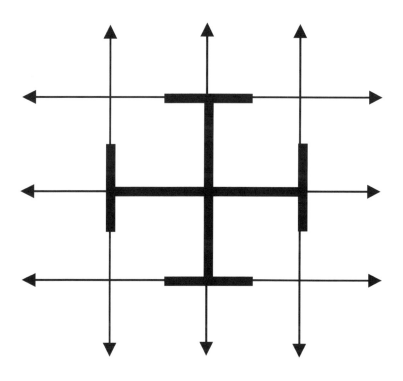

Thus we find 12 cubed or 12 X 12 X 12 truths (= 1728 truths) that are core to the wisdom and knowledge of the Magi priesthood. The core shape of the Magi cross is the simple cross with 4 lines or rays emanating out from a center point. At the end of each line is a perpendicular line of two rays with 8 rays as secondary to the core of the four. Together this portrays 12 rays of reality in many areas of truth.

The World of 12 We Live In

Twelve as a number is fully embedded into creation and is captured in the meaning of the Magi cross. Consider the following cycles and conditions of 12 found in nature and in society. These are only a few of the examples of 12.

- 12 constellations in the heavens.
- 12 celestial periods throughout all ages.
- 12 hours of day and 12 hours of night.
- 12 months of the year.
- 12 half steps on the chromatic scale of music in an octave.
- 12 chromatic colors of light in an octave of light..
- 12 as a numbering system common to the west - 12 inches to a foot. Also used by the Mayans.
- 12 tribes of Israel.
- 12 apostles as disciples of Jesus.
- 12 Commandments: 10 in the OT and 2 in the NT.
- 12 angelic captains over the 4 winds of nature.
- 12 toes and 12 fingers of the original Nephilim.
- 12 virtues of good and evil.
- 12 states of matter and energy.
- 12 dimensions of Space and Time or 12 dimensional realities.
- 12 areas of study for entering the Magi Priesthood.

Many of these 12's are obvious but some need further explanation and I will attempt to provide this in the following paragraphs with some examples.

12 Half-Steps in the Chromatic Scale of Music

The 12 half-steps in music are playing both the white keys and the black keys in sequence on the piano. If you begin on the C key, you would play the following notes:

1 C
2 C#
3 D
4 D#
5 E
6 F#
7 G
8 G#
9 A
10 A#
11 B
12 C

There are no half steps between B and C or between E and F so from C to C on the piano, it is 12 half steps.

12 Colors of Chromatic Light

When light is divided by a prism it provides normally 7 visible colors of light but for each color, there is a transitional color that is easily observed where one color phases into the next color of the seven. The full spectrum of chromatic colors of light are as follows:

1. red
2. red/orange
3. orange

4. orange/yellow
5. yellow
6. yellow/green
7. green
8. green/blue
9. blue
10. blue/indigo
11. indigo
12. purple or ultraviolet

When observing light, there is not a clear distinguishable transition color between indigo and purple so this has been left out.

12 Constellations and Eras of Time

The 12 constellations represent 12 different alien species with their alliances who have been granted 12 periods of time to influence the inhabitants of earth over the time of earth's long existence. The Creation of Adam as the 7th creation of humans on the present earth occurred after the last re-creation cycle of earth we see evident in the book of Geneses.

These 12 constellations originally reveal the full plan of YHWH in the creation of all things that in time will cycle back to him who is the beginning and the end of all things.

Sadly, astrology that was once used by the Three Kings to find their way to Y'Shua is now fully hijacked by the priests of the Serpent and can no longer be used as guidance. Simply, such knowledge has been lost through the ages that was likely once used by Noah, Enoch and lastly Shem.

Instead of the stars for guidance, we have been given a Holy Spirit by YHWH to lead and guide us into all truth. As beautiful as the stars are on a clear night, it is to the Holy Spirit we are to now look to for guidance and not to the stars.

We are currently in the era of Aquarius and as such find an 'aquarian' alien species now most connected with earth due to the alignment of this constellation to earth. What the means for earthlings is unknown to me at this time but may be revealed to me soon. I did have a dream recently where I had a conversation with great whale who seemed to embody a highly intelligent aquatic species.

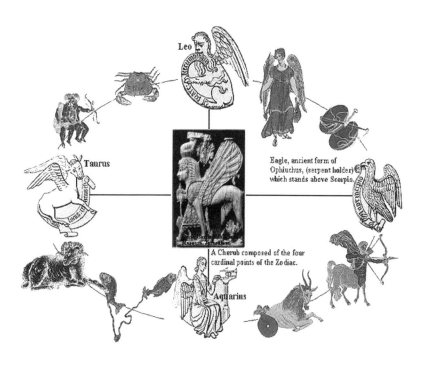

A Cherub composed of the four cardinal points of the Zodiac.

12 Content Areas of Learning

Of the 12 topics of study for the Magi priesthood, there are four rays as the core that represent truths in 1) Theology, 2) Philosophy, 3) Science and 4) Art.. The remaining 8 rays represent subsets of the four with the following under each. These again have 12 sub-sub sets of knowledge making learning for the Magi priesthood very extensive.

Under Theology in asking, "What is God?" there are the two rays of Creator and Savior from the perspective of God and his nature and ways. All areas of theology are spawned form this one question.

Theology What is God?	Philosophy What is Man?	Science What is Cosmos?	Arts What is Beauty?
Creator	Psychology	Creation	Design
Savior	Sociology	Mathematics	Aesthetics

In Philosophy in asking, "What is man?" is the study of man as a sole entity and man in relationships. There are minimally the two rays of Psychology and Sociology.

In Science in asking, "What is cosmos?" we find two rays in the study of Creation as filling space and Mathematics in measuring that space. The physical sciences and life science are a subsets of this question.

In the Arts in asking, "What is beauty?" there are the two rays of design and aesthetics which includes the graphic arts, music and theater. Each of these 12 can be divided again into at least 12 subsets. Only a few are mentioned here.

This is what modern colleges should be teaching broadly as a liberal arts curriculum and not the limited subject matter of professional trades that promise wealth and happiness but seldom deliver on this promise. I say this after 20 years of teaching in trade colleges as a professor.

You cannot really understand philosophy unless you understand theology. Science makes no sense unless you have both a theological and philosophical base to aid in interpreting the evidences of life and existence you see in nature. The value of all of these means nothing unless you have a core sense of aesthetics to decide if such knowledge is important to you or not. Does the knowledge have any real value?

Thus, the narrow focus of trade education today is pouring knowledge into the minds of students who have mental context 'holes' that let such knowledge run out because it has no personal meaning for them. Alas.... such is the perversion of American education.

I asked a class one time why they are going to college. Out of 25 students in my class, all but one said they were there to make more money. Their sole aesthetic was money in promising to provide more comfort and entertainment from a better paying job. I was amazed and also saddened.

12 Virtues of Good and Evil

Virtues are considered to be character traits that are consistently found in the life of a person. Many will equate these as perceived emotions and their following actions. In targeting the emotions, we can see two sets of six primary emotions one side being the good in contrast of the other considered to be undesirable.

- Love   vs.   Hate
- Faith   vs.   Fear
- Peace   vs.   Anger or unrest
- Joy   vs.   Sorrow
- Hope   vs.   Despair
- Humility   vs.   Pride

You will notice the positive virtues are commonly encouraged in the Holy Scriptures whereas the others are strongly discouraged.

12 States of Energy and Matter

Matter and energy are all made up of the same basic building blocks. Scientists are trying to figure out what this is and it is currently being called neutrinos having the smallest charge of all subatomic particles.

I would suggest the basic building block has an alternating negative and positive charge that cannot be detected with modern instruments. A very small merkaba building block.

However on the larger scale, most have discerned there are four states of change from matter in its conversion to energy. They include solids (earth), liquids (water), gas (wind or air) and, plasma (fire).

Each of these have three states of transitional being having to do with the amount of energy that is in motion then perceived as 'energy' and the amount of energy more are rest perceived as matter.

Water has the ability of transitioning through all 4 states without much difficulty. As ice, it is a solid, as water it is a liquid, as evaporated it becomes a gas and with the separation of hydrogen and oxygen, it can become an explosive plasma of fire like the sun. Adding to this the higher form of energy that is 4th dimensional and transitioning from plasma to scalar energy makes up the 12 transitional states of energy.

12 Dimensions of Reality

The 12 dimensions of reality is theoretical as very little of this has been observed and explained mathematically by science. It only remains in the grasping minds of out-of-the-box thinkers such as myself.

However, the following diagrams and explanations do provide a sense of how limited we are as humans being confined to the 3rd and 4th dimensional earth. We desire to reach out to understand realities far more diverse than our own but with earth binding dimensional limitations.

For many, the dream world and visions cross this barrier into the 4th and 5th dimensions. If a prophet is seeing into the future, they are crossing into the 6th dimension as described below. If you see YHWH (which is unlikely since the bible says no man can enter and live) you have entered into the 12th dimension of reality or YHWH has come down to you in your lower dimension which is more likely.

Let's take a look at the possible dimensions. Science has attempted to also make these distinctions but they limit themselves to time and space only and do not bring into the picture the idea if creating existence from nothing. In faith one can go beyond science and touch what science cannot touch.

FIRST DIMENSION: The dote represents the first level of reality. It is a point in space and has no time based reference to give it a sense of existence. It is there to be seen by other dimensions but cannot be seen by itself because it has no time as a reference to give it a sense of existence in time.

SECOND DIMENSION: Two dots connected by a line gives both space and time a place and thus a sense of existence. This is the simplest form of time and space that is the building blocks for all other dimensions. The line represents time whereas the two dots a separate point in space where one can 'see' the other to give itself a reference to claim existence. There is the possibility of simple self-awareness in this dimension but not much else.

THIRD DIMENSION: The simple box creates an area where within the boxed in area, there is coexistence in the same time and space for all entities within this reality. This is the primary animal-human reality where most people seem to exist. They only believe in what they can see and prove by the experience of the 5 senses that are limited to this dimension. This is sadly the world of modern science that has foolishly ignored the unexplainable and rejected it as a fringe para-science. The power in this realm is restricted to the limitation of the biological senses and limited power of the human mind and body.

FORTH DIMENSION: A cube represents a 4rd dimensional would in which some of the human creation now exists where there are experiences and things that cannot be seen or proven by the 5 senses but still are acknowledged to exist. A belief in God is a 4th dimensional reality in bridging a person from the animal constraints of the 3rd dimension into the spiritual or supernatural realm. It is in this reality that angels and demons are most commonly found and miracles and unexplainable events occur. The power is though the mind of faith that effects this realm.

FIFTH DIMENSION: Two cubes or separate realities interconnected with a common reference to time suggests two space-time realities interconnected at some distance. The string theory implies this in there being two realities distantly separated but still co-experiencing some common events in space and time. The relationship of YHWH and man is in the interconnect where the events in 'heaven' are linked to the events on earth. This could be as strong as a 'cause and effect' relationship where what happens in 'heaven' plays itself out on earth simultaneously.

SIXTH DIMENSION: Two cubes with a time disconnect (two vertical lines) suggests two separate time and space dimensions are interlinked in the support of time travel into the future and into the past. Experiments since the 1940's have been conducted in time travel or time displacement and have proven this is a reality. For prophets who seem to be able to see into the future, it is within this 6th dimension that this would be possible.

SEVENTH DIMENSION: This supposes the possibility of coexistence of a single entity in two or more realms or dimensions from a point in space where one would have the ability to express a presence in other realms all at the same time but not bound by any. This means an entity may co-exist in multiple dimensions all at the same time to interact with different species in each dimension. This would enable intercommunications between all of the dimensions that this entity would be experiencing at the same time. Angels as messengers seem to have this ability.

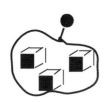 EIGHTH DIMENSION: This dimensional theory supposes an entity can be outside of all of a number of dimensions yet with a special relationship to these dimensions be able to manipulate the events within these dimensions as desired. Such species with this ability would be considered lessor 'gods' by the other dimensions below them in that they can change the sequence of events within their given control of dimensions.

 NINTH DIMENSION: This dimension supposes an entity has the power to create temporal life such as animals and man-like creatures that ceases to exist when their body dies. This human like being would not be an eternal soul but a temporal soul creation. These are formable 'gods' in the stronger sense of the term in claiming to be creators – even creators of some species of man. This is not genetic manipulation that can occur way down in the 3rd dimension and above but the creation of life from lesser energy sources drawing from all 9 dimensions.

 TENTH DIMENSION: This dimension supposes that an entity can create a soul with an eternal existence. Only YHWH has been known to be able to do this. When these creations die in body, their souls live on into eternity and some take on new bodies. Adam in the Garden of Eden was created with an eternal spirit-soul.

 ELEVENTH DIMENSION: This entity is able to create time and make time cease to exit or go backwards. Only YHWH can do this and that is why the prophecies of Revelation with the determined outcome is able to be commanded by YHWH. He holds the absolute power over time with respect to space.

TWELVTH DIMENSION: This is the ability to control all of space with respect to time and to create life from nothing anywhere and at anytime. It is the holding of absolute power over both time and space to make it exist or cease to exist. There is never really a state of nothing in the cosmos, there is always the will of Creator of all Creators (YHWH) who initiates all things from his own life force.

As we seek to better understand our relationship to the world around us and to the God YHWH who is the creator of all creators, we know the number 12 i8s fully integrated in the fabric of the creation of the cosmos and even in social institutions such as friends and family. Our mission in Messiah is to by faith function in all 12 of the dimensions presented here.

In John 17, Y'Shua prayed to YHWH for the church in saying, "May they all be one as you and I are one." This prayer is asking that we have the same unity with YHWH that Y'Shua has with YHWH as his first born son. If and when such a unity occurs for the rest of mankind, such a man or woman would then be called to function in all 12 of these dimensional worlds in doing the bidding of YHWH.

Chapter 25: Dream – Death Ray Weapon
Death Ray Threat

In the early morning of November 18th, 2012, I found my self in a multistory installation that appeared military in design and purpose with many military personnel present in the room. One of the officers in the room got the attention of the staff and told them they were being targeted with a 'death ray' and that they were not able to find a solution to shield themselves from its power.

They needed to assure this command center where they worked was protected as their main base of operations since it was vital to the success of the mission. I do not know who they were fighting but the impression is it was an alien species that had far more advanced technologies than what they had encountered before.

Caduceus Array

Silence reigned in the room and I waited to see what would happen. I waited for one of the scientists in the group to speak up with a technical solution but no one spoke. I finally blurted out that I knew how to make such a protected room and further said a caduceus coil array would be needed.

I then still dreaming sat down and designed the system with the caduceus coils set in an array to protect the command room as follows.

I began to explain about the characteristics of the Caduceus coil and why they would work in this situation.

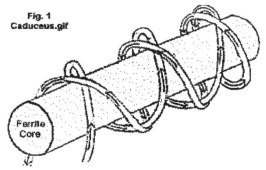

Fig. 1
Caduceus.gif

Ferrite Core

Since the caduceus coils have a very narrow field or spread focus of about 6 degrees, I would need an array of 8 coils in a room to create a standing wave that would cancel the death ray's microwave energy. The system would need very fast acting sensors that would identify the death ray energy and wavelength and then generate an opposite or negative signal of equal amplitude strength to cancel out the death ray frequencies.

The characteristics of the caduceus coils were tested and noted by William Smith who was the head of the Canadian Division of Transportation circa the 1950's. He stated in his papers that it was told to him that this design of coil "come from those from above" as stated in his working notes kept top secret until the 1990's. This of course suggests an alien origin for the design of the caduceus coil and not a human origin. He discovered the characteristics of the caduceus coils to perform as following:

1. There was no attenuation (reduction of signal) over the distances they measured.
2. It had about a 6 degree focus of beam from the end of the coil.
3. Signal appeared to travel at the speed of light and was not effected by mass or environment.
4. There was no internal resistance in the coil so very small wires could be used for very high power loads. The coil never heated up.
5. There was no need to tune the coils since it seemed to be equally efficient at all frequencies tested.

Caduceus Metal Fusion

I then found myself in the dream holding a small hand-held device also based on the caduceus coil that would send out a directional ray and heat up all metals and cause them to be too hot to handle.

I aimed the device at a metal object with metal moving parts and I then saw sparks start to arc between the moving parts of the object. It was apparent the caduceus ray would act as an arc welder and fuse all of the moving parts together. This small hand held device could make all metal based weapons with metal moving parts totally useless in battle I thought to myself in amazement.

I then saw a glimpse of a battle where all of the guns, vehicles, tanks, missile launchers and more that were on the battle field made of metals were totally useless and men were then seen swinging their guns in hand to hand combat while holding the plastic and wood butts of their guns.

All transport vehicles were suddenly motionless and quiet. Nothing with a metal part that moved against another metal part was working. All were fused together by the caduceus ray but it did not seem to harm the soldiers.

Non-Metallic Weapons

Then the scene changed again and I saw the quick development of non-metallic machines using ceramics, plastics and compressed wood fiber materials to then be used in a future battles. I watched a battle occur and the materials of these vehicles were like coal and once on fire, they burned like coal. These combustible fiber based vehicles were not hard to catch on fire so they too failed over time as the battle continued.

Horseman and Swords

The scene then changed for the last time in the dream and I saw horsemen with some kind of swords – perhaps ceramics that were now used in battle near the end of these ongoing world wars. Only the best swordsmen were able to survive in battle as the once advanced technologies that were boasted by the nations became useless. I then awoke.

Commentary

Many years ago, I heard the Russian made tanks from compressed wood fiber. It was stronger and lighter than steel but it burned like coal. I am not aware that it has ever been used in any of the Russian military campaigns.

This does show that non-metallic technology is known for vehicle frames and bodies. Engines can be made from ceramics however most heat resistant ceramics have metal in them so there would need to be a new technology of engines yet undiscovered.

This dream aligns with scripture where it says that in the Battle of Armageddon, the blood lying over the Valley of Megeddo will be up the horses bridle from the men who have died in this final battle. This would only occur if severe bloodletting weapons were used such as swords.

Further, it suggests there will be a level playing field in the end times battle so it will not be advanced technologies that win the final war but the faith and skill of the men fighting in hand to hand combat who will be the victors.

It also says that "he who picks up the sword will die by the sword" in the last days. Perhaps this is saying that all godly people should resolve to be prophets and take up sticks (a staff) for battle and let YHWH with his angelic armies win the wars against the Antichrist of the future? However, if we fight with the sword at the coming of Messiah Y'Shua who will come also with a sword, it is his battle we are fighting and not our own and we know he will be victorious.

Chapter 26: Steam Motorcycle Reborn
Why Steam?

Steam is one of the most easily captured renewable resources and the engine can be built with off the shelf components. The choice of steam for motorcycles has a very long history and was used before gas fuel became popular or even the gas engine was invented. I would guess it was the oil companies that pushed fossil fuels upon the world as steam was powered from burning wood or coal that often could be found locally. Certainly wood is a renewable resource and would be the optimum choice for a near "FREE" fuel for the vehicle.

Some of the earliest steam bikes circa the 1850's were nothing more than bone crusher bikes with steam boilers and engines added. However the simplicity and efficiency of the design then has not changed much as 'steam bike' builders today adapt a comfortable bicycle frame and add a more efficient boiler and engine.

I like the idea of steam driven vehicles and combining it with the new developments of gasification of biomass may be just what the world is looking for. Gasifier technologies have found ways to burn biomass so completely that there is virtually no smoke or particulates put into the air. It is a cleaner burn than gas engines. I worked for a while with the biomass Energy Foundation in Golden, Colorado as a Research Engineer in developing new technologies for gasification.

Gasifiers

The gasifiers that were built there were able to run an 8 cylinder Ford engine and generate 10KW of electricity from Asai seeds which are like wood pellets. The organization even invented a simple portable wood burning down-draft cook stove (right) that produces a blue flame to cook on for camping using wood you would find in the forest.

The little stove uses a small fan that runs for hours and a single battery but this could be remedied with the addition of a small bicycle generator used for head lights but in this case used to charge a small lithium battery.

In the development of the next generation of steam bikes, I would take current design and add little $29 cook stove and adapt it to boil water to produce steam to drive the motorcycle. If the design used wood pellets as its fuel and then employed an auger to keep adding fuel at a set rate to keep the fire intense, water boiling and steam coming, we would likely have a very reliable steam boiler system that can consistently produce steam.

The next challenge would be to adapt an air or steam engine that is light weight and can be located on the steam bike to optimize power to the wheels. There are a number of companies that are producing a positive displacement vane engine that can turn at any RPM with out any loss of efficiency. These are very high torque engines and run at very high efficiencies. If such an engine were integrated into the back hub of the motorcycle, this would be a grand little steam bike to be driving in the city and on the byways.

The use of a robust bicycle frame for the vehicle rather than the heavier motorcycle frame is advised. This would likely be the reasonable choice for future steam powered bicycles for inner city driving in the moped category. However for highway driving, all would have to be upscaled for higher speeds and higher power output.

Since steam powered engines can be designed near silent, this would be great for inner city driving. When you get low on fuel, just stop by your local hardware or grocery store and pick up another bag of wood pellets normally sold for wood pellet heating systems and pour them into the hopper for another hundred miles or more. Happy steaming down the road!

Chapter 27: Return to 19th Century Aether Energy
Feeble Attempt at Alternative Energy

We are coming into a time when fossil fuels and even conventional alternative energy systems will come under the complete control of the NWO. Solar voltaics are still very inefficient and most that pay to have a system installed for them seldom gain a return on their investment over a 15 year period.

There is much that can be read about 'over-unity' energy systems. Over unity means that you get more energy out of a system than what you put into it because it is drawing excess energy from ambient energy called Aether in the 19th century that exists everywhere in the universe. There is no such thing as a complete vacuum in space nor can it be created by man in a lab. The density of this ambient Aether energy is 97,000 times more dense than matter yet we walk through it completely unaffected every day.

Return to the 19th Century

Tesla, Worrlie, Keely and others just before the turn of the 19th century experimented extensively with this Aether energy and built devices that were able to capture this illusive energy to power vehicles, levitate masses, make massive stone quartz turn into powder in seconds, make very small aether generators for electricity and even approach harnessing atomic energy without the radioactive fallout that is common today.

We have become more dumb in our sciences since the 19th century as the NWO system would make sure these devices were never commercialized for us for the common household. We might call this energy terrorism in withholding vital energy designs that wold make Americans completely independent on government and corporate energy systems. The fact is, we need this free energy to avoid becoming slaves.

Energy Needed to Avoid Slavery

It is time to revisit these patents and existing devices and based on current technology capabilities, begin to build and disperse these devices to those who will not bow before the idols of the NWO as promoted by the Jesuits (NWO Army Command), the Illuminati (World Bankers/Financiers) and the Priory of Sion (Black or hidden Royals).

This trinity of powers are avowed Luciferians and know that if humanity can be completely self-sufficient from their control of energy, they will be able to control all in due time. This fact makes it paramount that we as the called out ones rediscover the Aether energy and immediately develop systems that can capture this energy for the remnant who are faithful to YHWH.

Healing For the Saints

Healing comes in many ways and is not just limited to the body but is also a healing of the soul and the human spirit. Since who we are is all interconnected, what happens to us spiritually or emotionally will often express itself in our bodies in the form of illness.

In this section, I first tell the story of my major brush with death that at the time of this writing was only 9 weeks ago so it is still very fresh in my mind. I will share some dreams I have had on healing and how the study of bioenergy is very important to understand in the art and science of healing. I will then venture into the world of love to discuss how true love can heal what no drug or potion can heal.

If I was to extend this section which should be done, I would add many chapters on the healing capabilities of herbs. This I think should be a separate book since it is so extensive and each geographic area has a different collection of healing herbs that wold have to be researched.

There is a book on the healing herbs found in the high Rockies which is right for this area, but little information is in the book on how to prepare the various remedies. This may be a future book I should write that would complement this NWO series.

Chapter 28: Dream – The Garden of Our Souls
Heart Attacks at 10,000 Feet

As I remember back to the early days of my youth, I know I have been called to share the word of YHWH to the people of YHWH.   Many times I have faced the powers of darkness who desire to shorten my life before its time.

In the early part of April 2013, I began to feel chest pains, shortness of breath and fatigue.   I lived at Saint Michaels Abbey which is really no more than a construction trailer and canvas storage dome located in the geological quadrangle of Glentivar near Hartsel, Colorado. The elevation of the Abbey was near 10,000 feet elevation where the air is thin and rises up from there onto 1.2 millions acres of Pike National Forest to the East. I lived in the frontier wilderness of the Colorado Rockies where my closest neighbor was over a mile away.

For the last two years, I had not been able a secure a reliable vehicles so hitch hiking has become a normal mode of travel for me.   As I stood by the road side in the 4th of April with my arm stretched out with thumb pointing to the East, again I felt the tightening of my chest, sharp pains go down my left arm and a shortness of breath.

What should I do I wondered with some desperation. Cars only pass about every 10-15 minutes in this remote area and in recent years, fear has gripped the hearts of most Americans in greatly eroding the American sense of helping their fellow man.

After an hour of seeking a ride, I realized that my condition was not getting any better and I called a friend who lives more like a mountainman than one in civilized society. He agreed to come down out of the mountain and drive me the 35 miles to the closest city of Woodland Park to the little hospital there.

Upon arrival at the hospital, I was placed on a stretcher and after 5 minutes of tests they said I was having a series of heart attacks and they immediately rolled me into an awaiting ambulance to be taken to Memorial Hospital 25 miles further to the East in Colorado Springs. I was gone before my mountainman friend could find out what was my condition.

Being Probed

At Memorial now in the Emergency Unit, a prob was run up the artery in my right leg into my heart. The doctors discovered two of the heart arteries were totally blocked and a third mostly blocked. I was then told again I was having a series of heart attacks and that triple bypass open heart surgery was required. Since I had only one kidney with the other missing due to a birth defect, they were concerned. Even the good kidney they said was only working at about 30-50% and that bypass surgery would likely destroy what is left of this function leaving me to endure kidney dialysis the rest of my life.

`The doctors stabilized me and decided to wait a day before surgery to try to bring back more of the function of the one kidney. In recent years, this low function of the remaining kidney has resulted in bouts of severe gout lasting for months at times and continuous arthritis in the knees and hands.

On the 5th of April, I was taken into the Operating Room at Memorial with multiple doctors attending. I do not remember much of this since I was 'put to sleep' for the surgery. However, it is at this time that I began to see and experience what was later called in my dreams and visions by both forces of light and darkness as the "Garden of the Soul."

Battle of Light and Darkness

The first experience was in watching the battle of light against darkness. The entity of darkness appeared to have a soul of its own yet it needed light or life energy from  other entities to sustain its existence. It was a parasite entity sucking the life from the dying. I saw it at different locations in the room as a black mist that looked like moving coal dust that was about 12″ wide by 12″ long 6″ tall. It had eyes and was in constant motion as the black coal mist of its composition bubbled up around itself.

I most often saw it nestled on the shelf just beyond the foot of my bed watching me. It would float in to the air and approach me in the night to try to 'suck' my life from me but a white light from above would suddenly appear and drive it back into the dark recesses of the room. I saw this happen over and over again both during the surgery and immediately after the surgery

My sense is that this dark mist was not wholly evil of itself but had sometime in the past made the wrong decisions and thus had inadvertently disconnected itself from the white light source of life and now it survives by capturing the remaining life force from others of greater energy so it can sustain a very remedial level of existence.

It may have had a body at one time. It may have been a human or some other kind of soul that had lost its way and now is at the verge of being fully 'snuffed' out. It now barely survives existing like a vampire living off of the life energy of others who are not protected by the white light.

The white light in this experience is the light of YHWH. Whether you want to call this the light of the Holy Spirit, the light of truth that liberates and protects, it all comes from the same source, YHWH.

The First Garden

As the days past after the surgery, I was first shown by YHWH the garden of my soul. Sadly, it was very desolate and one could not really call it a garden. It was a floating garden but there was little or no water in this garden. It displayed many different plants in various stages of life …. or really death. In my garden there were small man-made miniature buildings scattered among the dying plants which were my attempts in life to do 'good' for God. They did not grow – they just took up space.

I realized that I had very little to show in my life that would carry into eternity. My garden was floating next to the gardens of the others I called close friends and they all were shaped in a hexagonal pattern like a Honey comb with each garden I saw having 6 sides. The closest gardens connected to others were our closest relationships such as parents, wife or husband, children, siblings and close friends. In my case, their gardens were also mixed with life and death.

I then was told that "**as your garden is nurtured, the gardens next to yours will also be nurtured.**" The facts is as I looked, they were not being nurtured. It seemed the more I tried to do 'good' in the sight of YHWH, the worse my garden became and the worse the gardens connected to mine became. I was very sad about this since I love my family. I asked YHWH in this visitation what I should do.

The New Garden of my Soul

I was then told, **"the garden of your soul will nurture itself if you will let it occur."** Nurture itself? How is this possible? I then saw my old garden disappear and a new garden emerge now floating where the old garden had once existed. In this new garden, I saw 7 floating metallic bowls full of rainbow light and sound that was composed of both light and water in the form of a life-giving heavy mist flowering form one into the other like a dry ice mist.

I saw the light of all of the colors of the rainbow in my new garden. It seemed right that since my physical heart had been refurbished with a triple bypass, that my garden of the soul should also have a new start. I understood that these bowls were now in place to hold the water that was missing in my self-nurtured garden.

As I watched, I could see the different bowls pour their 7 colors of light-music mist from one into the other as they constantly moved about in the garden. As they poured into the others, music was heard – a very peaceful music that quiets even the deepest distresses of the soul. I knew immediately that this was the music of creation that can make something new from just the power of faith and love.

I then began to see life miraculously sprout from the garden – many different kinds of plants started to grow that had not been planted. I realized that where ever there was pure light, there would be pure life and gardens growing. I remembered that the seven colors of the rainbow when combined make pure white light.

As I stood back and watched my new garden of the soul begin to grow, I suddenly began to cry and said to myself, "Now I had a garden of the soul that was alive and eternal – would last forever!" It was clear I was not to plant my 'good' works in this new garden but just live each day to bring life to others and YHWH would plant and nurture what is needed in my garden.

One day I tried to bring a little bush to my garden but I was then told by YHWH, **"Just a little leaven will leaven the whole lump."** I thought for a moment than realized this meant don't bring your own stuff to the garden, let YHWH plant what is needed in the Garden of your Soul. I then just set the little plant to the side and continued to watch my garden grow.

Turning Back the Darkness

I then saw an intense white light come to hover over my garden. In the distance, I noticed the dark mist was trying to sneakily approach my new garden of the soul to cause mischief.

The white light responded in pulsating with light and music in energizing the 7 colors enabling them to push back the death attack of the mist of darkness.

I was then told by YHWH, **"The life now in the garden of your soul flows over into your body in healing. As your soul is healed, so will your body also be healed."**

I then knew what is needed with this capstone message from YHWH. As we give ourselves fully to YHWH and cease from our own 'good' works, he then will nurture our garden and protect it from the curses of the mists of darkness. When our garden of the soul is nurtured, so will the gardens of those around us who are loved by us will be nurtured.

I also realized from this 'death and resurrection' experience that my heart was changed from a heart of stone (hardened and blocked arteries) to a heart of flesh. It is now my life's task to work with other light workers to encourage the needy to 'let go and let YHWH' nurture the garden of their souls. If many can learn to do this, they will have another chance at life in extending their physical life span rather then dying prematurely.

Hospice Mission

This new mission for me may take on the form of a Hospice ministry where I work with others – each with their own gardens - sharing together in the task of providing Hospice facilities to the dying and chronically ill.

I believe as we pursue the white light of YHWH, the art of balancing the 7 colors of healing for the body associated with the endocrine system along with this music of healing will be revealed to us. It would be my hearts desire to sing the songs of healing and see the dying come to new life and live.

I was lastly told by YHWH that, **"many patients who come across your path will find peace from the torment within their souls and many will be healed even though deemed terminally ill by Western medicine."** I now believe this to be true.

If this story has touched you deeply and you feel a calling to become a healing brother or sister or would like to work with us as an intern, please contact Abbot David Michael directly. Let's explore this healing mission together to bring life to many who would otherwise die prematurely.

Chapter 29: Bioenergy Healing for the Church and the World

Introduction

Bioenergy healing has been developed in many cultures and was known to excel in the most ancient cultures of Asia (Chinese), Western Europe (Celts), India (Brahmans), N. America (Anasazi), S. America (Mayans / Aztecs) and the Fertile Crescent (Sumeria → Babylon → Egypt → Greece → Rome).

These cultures did pass on some of what they discovered yet with much moire forgotten. Sadly, it has been the tendency of western society to give less credibility to the naturalpathic arts while the drug companies of our day claim the supremacy of science in their proposed remedies yet they limit themselves to the drug and cut approach.

The downside of most of the highly concentrated drugs today are the side effects that are in some cases only slightly less deadly than the dis-ease they were invented to remedy. If you listen carefully to the TV ads on new drugs, death is often listed s a possible side effects of the drug. Surely there is a better approach and there is. It has been shown that $1/4^{th}$ of all of those who die in hospitals after a procedure die due to the side effects of prescribed drugs.

Naturopathy Defined

There are seven optional naturalpathic therapies in the field of bioenergy healing available in the medical bag for well-trained naturalpathic doctors. The term naturalpathic is defined as:

Source: On-line Dictionary

Naturopathy is a system or method of treating disease that employs no surgery or synthetic drugs but uses special diets, herbs, vitamins, massage, etc., to assist the natural healing processes.

Source: The American Association of Naturalpathic Physicians

Naturalpathic medicine is a distinct system of primary health care - an art, science, philosophy and practice of diagnosis, treatment and prevention of illness. Naturalpathic medicine is distinguished by the principles which underlie and determine its practice.

These principles are based upon the objective observation of the nature of health and disease, and are continually reexamined in the light of scientific advances. Methods used are consistent with these principles and are chosen upon the basis of patient individuality. Naturalpathic physicians are primary health care practitioners, whose diverse techniques include modern and traditional, scientific and empirical methods.

The Seven Therapies of Naturopathy

What we can surmise from these definitions is that naturopathy is first a philosophy of approach with extensive remedy options that are chosen based on the needs of the individual as a custom designed combination of remedies to re-balance the biological energy fields of the mind and body.

The seven optional bioenergy therapies include bioelectrics, bio-acoustic, biomagnetics, biophotonics, biochemism, biothermism and biokenisthetics.

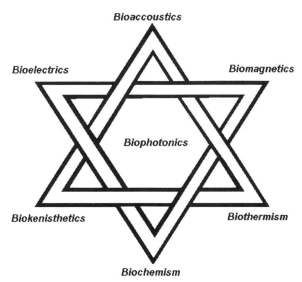

What is interesting about all of these therapies is they are just different expression of energy found in different spectrums with different intensities of frequencies. Chemicals (drugs), light, magnetics, heat, sound, and pressure all give off a set chord of specific pulsed frequencies so they are really just a different expression of the same energy we call bioenergy as the energy that sustains all life.

Musical Form Found Within All Energy

In my opinion the study of music and harmonics is foundational to understanding bioenergy as one translates the model of the musical octave and its chordal harmonics to these seven other energy forms. In the late 19th century, Maslow discovered the elements on the periodic table were one octave apart if the resonate frequencies of these elements were square rooted and compared starting with fundamental element of Hydrogen.

The genius Keely also of the late 19th century discovered that all of the 7 known expressions of energy were just different spectral groupings on a massive energy continuum starting with heavy matter (chemism) and continuing through the 4th dimensional energy dimension that we call the spirit realm.

Five Senses

We define these energy expressions primarily with our 5 senses. Biochemism (drugs) is within the realm of the sense of taste and smell while also effecting our bodily digestive system, skin or blood when taken intravenously or applied locally. Biophotonics (light) is within sensory the realm of our sight. Bioacoustics is within the realm of our sense of hearing, Bioelectics, Biomagnetics, Biokinesthetics and Biothermism are within the realm of our bodies sense of feel, touch and pressure.

The fact is all that exists in creation, seen and unseen, can be explained in terms of energy as we witness its effects based on its respective spectrum of sensory impact as a part of the infinite energy continuum. This is the real 'unified field theory' that has evaded most Western scientists. Even God (YHWH) is explain in the Bible as an "all consuming fire [an energy form of the highest frequencies] in which no man can enter and live." Let's now consider the seven expressions of bioenergy.

Bioelectrics

This field of bioenergy is known as pulsed electrical energy therapy. In this approach, pulsed electrical energy is strategically focused on certain parts of the body to effect a positive balance of electrical energy in the body.

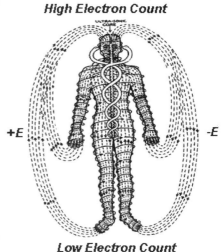

High Electron Count

+E   -E

Low Electron Count

It is known that our head has far more electrons per square inch than your feet resulting from the electrons in the sky passing through your conductive body to the ground. Your left side (hand) has a negative potential compared to your right side so if you held the two wires of a very sensitive volt meter, you would show an electric polarity and voltage difference. You are in effect a living battery. During a lightening storm if you were standing outside, your head can be over 1000 volts higher in electrical potential than your feet.

Within this polarity of human voltage, there are many frequencies alternating within the body that keep the cells functioning according to the electrically mapped design of the DNA within those cells. When outside electrical frequencies oppose the natural frequencies and pulse of the DNA in the cells, the cells then loose their sense of identity and become cancerous and then unknowingly oppose the frequencies and pulse of the other cells round them. To provide the correct set of electrical pulsed frequencies to the weakened cells will energize them to return to their original design.

Work in the 1940s with pulsed electrical energy with cancer patients has proved to be effective in causing cancer cells to revert back to their original purpose as mapped into the DNA of these cells. However, the drug companies in America who control the FDA have banned these healing technologies for the last 75 years.

Bioelectric therapy tends to be more surface since electricity tends to not penetrate the skin unless in higher amperage's which may cause problems like electrocution and death. For deep tissue therapies the alternative of biomagnetics is often chosen instead of bioelectrics.

Bioacoustics

This field of bioenergy is known as sound energy therapy. There are seven notes in the diatonic scale (like C major scale) with the octave making an 8 note scale. There are 11 notes in the Chromatic scale with the added octave making 12 notes.

The body is very susceptible to music frequencies both through hearing and through the sensory 'feeling' of these frequencies upon the body. All cells in the body have a set or chord of frequencies that are mapped by the DNA for that cell.

Some researchers have suggested that DNA is no more than resonating bio-antennas (between the two strands of the DNA) that receive and send out sets of frequencies to their host cells to cause them to perform specific functions in the body. When music is played as a set of frequencies and is in sympathetic frequency (tuned) with the natural positive resonate frequencies of the cells, it becomes a form of entrainment that positively energizes the cells to function more fully in their designed capacity.

When foreign elements (chemicals) or frequencies (high power lines, etc) are imposed in or upon the body close to and even in the cells, this negative opposing energy is often observed to be carcinogenic in producing their own set of frequencies that through entrainment overcome the weakened DNA frequencies and take over the natural function of the cells causing dis-ease and ill-health.

Music in our audible hearing range is much lower than the frequencies of the cells but when a note or chord is played, there are harmonics or higher semitones generated that go up into the spectrum of light from music and will directly impact the cells in their respective bioenergy spectrum.

For this reason, one should be careful about the music they listen to and be assured such music does not provide frequencies that oppose or weaken the natural functions of the human mind and body.

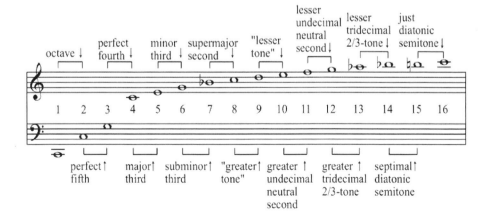

Music is built on the idea of a fundamental tone which is reinforced by the octave and other frequencies. The natural harmonic series includes the Octave, 5th, 4th, 3rd, etc. See chart above.

These are the basic building blocks for consonant (pleasant sounding) chords with healing tones as built upon the natural harmonic intervals of the 3rd, 4th, 5th and so on. Is it generally consonant chords (harmonic tones) that support good cell function. Dissonant chords tend to cause stress upon the body and its cells.

Along with the well-trained full resonate voice, there are certain instruments that have been proven to be more effective in music therapy due to the natural timbre of these instruments. The harp (strings), flute (woodwinds) and tuned bells (percussion) all have the characteristic of effecting the least amount of compression (distortion) on the sound wave thus more closely imitating the natural sounds found in nature and in the human body.

Bioacoustics is a therapy field that needs much more research and testing. It is a mode of healing that is accessible by most anyone who can carry a tune or play an instrument. The human voice alone can be the instrument of healing so you carry this instrument with you at all times.

Biomagnetics

This field of bioenergy is know as magnetic energy therapy. As mentioned above, biomagnetics is a deep penetrating bioenergy that will go through the skin deep into the muscle tissue for remedying weaker cells.

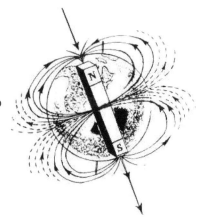

The north pole of magnetism has a 'drawing out' (vacuum) effect on energy whereas the south pole of magnetism has a 'putting in' (pressure) effect on energy. If you want to put positive bioenergy into the body, you can place a 'remedy' on the surface of the area to be healed and have the magnet placed between the remedy and the body with the southern (negative) pole facing towards the body. If you want to draw out negative energy from the body to weaken this energy, you would place the northern pole of the magnetic toward the skin.

Magnetism has been used to help with arthritis to lessen pain and reduce swelling. If one knows the frequency set of the cells that need healing, using pulsed electromagnets to provide a life healing magnetic pulse to strengthen the weak cells may remedy the problem all together as the cells are repaired.

It should also be noted here that there is likely other reasons why these cells became weak and a naturalpathic doctor needs to look at the whole system of the body to identify and stop the cause of the problem rather than just treat the symptoms.

Biophotonics

This field of bioenergy is known as the 7-color visible light energy therapy. These seven colors are evident in the natural division of light caused by a prism and seen s the colors of the rainbow.

The seven colors are red, orange, yellow, green, blue, indigo and violet. These colors correspond to the seven notes of the diatonic scale with similar energy effects upon the body.

Light therapy is sometimes used projected into the eyes to then cause the brain to translate these energy frequency colors into chemical-electric signals that effect the hormonal endocrine system within the body. Sometimes a room will be filled with specific light spectrums to enhance or reinforce the frequencies that are deficient in the body to enhance the natural healing process. Light projected on the skin has also shown to effect the body in healing.

Different colors can easily create moods upon the mind and have been used to help those with mental disorders to find a more even temperament in dealing with life's many challenges.

Chakra Diagnostics

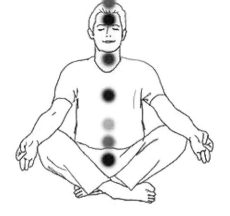

The observation of the aura which is the body emanating various spectrums of light of low intensity (not easily visible except by sensitive practitioners) has been used for medical diagnostics in identifying the energy deficiencies in the body.

These deficiencies are often traced to specific organs and systems in the body that need attention.   The 7 Chakras of the body associated with the endocrine system are often assigned certain light colors. These colors are the dominate color frequencies in which the various endocrine systems of the body function.

Biochemism

This field of bioenergy is known as employing chemical drugs - both naturalpathic and synthetic drugs including aromatic and 'tea' therapies. This is the most developed therapy used by conventionally trained medical doctors in America. In modern medicine, it is largely a cut and drug scenario where synthetic drugs are used because they are very fast acting.

The down side is they often have side effects that negatively impact the other areas of the body. In contrast, natural remedies are often slower acting but seem to have less side effects.

Some will argue that the active ingredient in a synthetic drug as compared to the same active ingredient in a natural drug cannot be differentiated by the human body. This is likely true for the active ingredient but naturally produced and gathered drugs have innumerable other natural additives and trace elements that seem to reduce the negative impact of the active ingredient in the natural form. Also the active ingredient is normally in much lower doses so it does not overwhelm the system.

Naturalpathic remedies are often grown in herb gardens as a supplement to food. Other forms of administering remedies is in concocted natural teas and aroma therapy where the remedy is put into the air in the form of steam or scent.

The old vaporizers we as kids slept with with Vicks remedies were a solid approach in administering chemical remedies like the Native American Sweat lodges. Much work has been done in almost every culture in identifying locally found herbal remedies for most anything that ails you .

Biothermism

The field of bioenergy is known as heat therapy in the application of static and pulsed infrared heat to different parts of the body. Heat therapy is common when using an electrical 'heating pad' on your back when going to sleep. Heat tends to loosen the muscles and the heat also draws more oxygen carrying blood to the area to more quickly facilitate a relaxation and healing the stressed or damaged muscles.

Some research has been conducted in pulsing the heat to match the natural frequencies of the human body. Heating pads are powered usually by 60 cycle AC voltage which is not conducive to the natural frequencies of the human body.

A better heating device would be a DC heating pad or one designed to the Schumann resonance of earth which is about 7.8 cycles per second. This would be true for all devices that carry the 60 cycle frequency or the household electrical system into the human body.

Biokinesthetics

This field of bioenergy is known as employing pressure in the form of various techniques of massage therapy. There are many techniques developed in various countries where the muscles are manipulated in such a manner to remove tension and to add heat through friction to enhance blood flow and healing.

I must say a good massage is the answer to many common physical stress conditions but it would be a wise decision to identify the cause of the stress and prevent it from happening in the first place.

In addition to muscle relaxation, there are pressure points on the human body that can effect relation. Some of the pressure point areas include the temples on the sides of the  head and neck, erotic pressure points or zones on the body and the use of reflexology that has mapped pressure points all over the body used in healing.

Meridian Systems

The bodies meridian systems is still largely unknown to most of Western medicine in that it has not been fully accepted as a viable biological system in the body. It is a parallel system to the nervous and endocrine system but carries an energy form that is closer to light and magnetics rather than chemical-electrical impulses.

The meridian system is not directly effected by the use of drugs unless the drugs have added energy that pushes their frequency output into the light range. Heat and burning (fire) of chemical (natural or synthetic) remedies is a common way to do this.

The Chinese have developed system maps of the human body showing the meridian lines that are used in reflexology, acupressure, acupuncture and other Eastern healing methods. The meridian lines connect parts and systems in the body to end points (triggers or access points) found on the hands and feet and on other parts of the body to specific organs and body systems.

It has been discovered that the glands of the human body within the endocrine system and brain have 'bio-crystalline' materials such a iron ferrite that is known to have peizo characteristics. When activated, they generate frequencies up into the visible light spectrum and above.

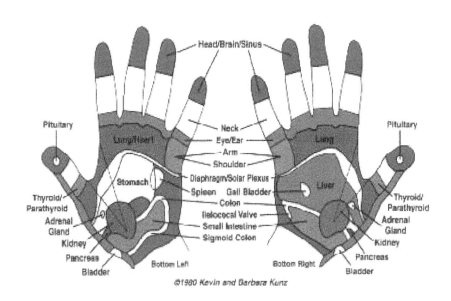

©1990 Kevin and Barbara Kunz

It is thought that the meridian system transmits these ultra-high frequency signals to all parts of the body in reaching frequencies within the 'spiritual' spectrum of energy. Thus the human body can be healed through prayer and other spiritual rituals as found evident in many different religions.

The use of the meridian system has been targeted for the development of health diagnostic electronics in determining the frequency deficiencies of specific parts of the human body. It has also been used to transmit all of the 7 bioenergies to specific areas of the body for healing.

Final thoughts

There is a great need for Naturalpathic doctors to be trained to address the health needs of the Church and the world. As soon as we are born, we start dying even though we are observed to be growing up into adulthood.

Sadly, there has been a change in the environment of earth since the Garden of Eden by the coming of the great flood that greatly reduced the life span of humans from the average of 400 to 500 years down to about 70 to 90 years.

The direct cause of this was the reduction in earth's air pressure reducing our oxygen intake to half of what is needed for sustained cell regeneration. In addition, the once protecting layer of water (ocean) in the sky above is now gone and no longer filters out the harmful rays of the sun and outer space like a massive green house.

However, we can endeavor to listen to the signs of our body in identifying the cause of its dis-ease and illness. We can then give it what it needs in the form one or more of the seven bioenergies that will keep it functioning well until we are done with our spiritual journey on this earth.

Chapter 30: Healing by Magnetic Music
Music in Healing

In preaching the simplicity of the Gospel, it would be good to keep the dying alive long enough so they can accept Y'Shua as Lord and Savior before they breath their last breath.

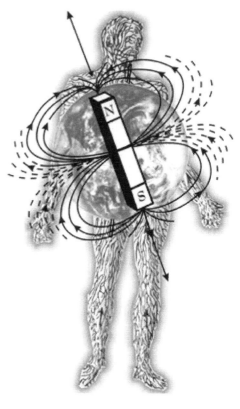

Some years ago, I was a graduate assistant to a professor at the University of Hawaii that was developing music that would heal. What makes sense in all this is that all of creation including matter has now been proven to be just a set of atomic level frequencies held together because they are in harmony.

Even the atom is not a solid ball of matter but a very small density of energy like an atomic cloud that is both vibrating within itself and is also resonating with respect to other atomic densities of energy to form molecules. Every chemical can be duplicated by the sounding of a set of frequencies. Matter can even be made to appear or disappear from nowhere from the 'aether' or the invisible energy in all of space with the right frequencies. There is no such thing as an absolute vacuum in space. Pulsating energy is everywhere and cannot be avoided.

Even tastes and smells are just a set of frequencies characteristic of the elemental chemicals that are within a substance. There is a simple formula that identifies what the frequency is for each element. This is not rocket science but really just an extended form of basic music theory. Some have said that if you study music theory, you have actually studied the fundamental concepts of the most challenging frontiers of nuclear physics.

When the body is healthy, all parts are resonating at their God assigned frequencies and are literally in harmony (sympathetic resonance) with each other. When the body is ill, it is because there are harmful frequencies sounding within the body. Even cancer is just an action of the wrong frequencies sounding in the body that cause healthy cells to in time, begin to take on the sound in resonance with the cancer causing agents. This is called entrainment.

Music Within Y'Shua

When Y"Shua healed, he would touch people and pass on into their bodies the rightful frequencies that were needed to set right and heal the areas in need. When the woman with the issue of blood touched Jesus, he said, "Who touched me" and that he felt energy (virtue) leave his body toward whomever touched him. This was the rightful frequencies leaving his body to re-tune the cells in the woman's body that was causing the issue of blood. She was then miraculously healed.

Chinese Doctor

While teaching sensor electronics at Heald College in Hawaii and doing a side work with DAARPA (Aerospace R&D), I was asked to assist a Chinese doctor who had invented a device that would take a pill or Chinese organic remedy and transfer that chemical set of frequencies electrically to infuse it into plane water.

Yes... just plain water. Water is the atomic composition of hydrogen and oxygen and can be tuned to almost any other set of frequencies that compose the elements in the Periodic Table. Hydrogen in particular has a frequency that is the base or root frequency to all other elements so to tune hydrogen is to simply add overtones or harmonics to the existing frequencies of hydrogen to become effectively other elements. Research in this area dates to the end of the 19th century with Keely, Tesla and others who through experimentation, proved the healing nature of music frequencies.

BioMagnetics

We could choose to use electricity, sound (ultrasound), magnetics or light to tune water as a remedy but the most effective appears to be magnetics. Magnetics is able to penetrate the natural resistance of the water to tune every molecule within whereas electricity, light and sound are deflected or are filtered by the water. In order to better understand the electrically induced biomagnetics approach to healing, it is necessary to study the Meridian energy lines of the human body as common to the practice of Eastern medicine.

The Meridian lines and Acupuncture points seem to be effective in transferring healing energy directly into the specific organs and systems of the body. To just ingest the chemicals or the remedy frequencies (chemicals), the chemicals will be distributed by the blood system and affect all organs and systems.

Such a 'shotgun' approach may and does cause additional toxic problems which is the case with many common drug based healing methods. Chemotherapy is often the cause of death and not the cancer. This is barbaric in my opinion.

Diagnostics

This same Chinese doctor also used a modified reverse of the system to test for illness in the body by testing energy levels at each Meridian point that connects to all of the various organs and systems of the body.

If the system was at rest or in harmony (in balance), the energy level needed to sustain the balance was low. However, if the organ or system was distressed, the energy level or activity was high due to the conflict or dissonance of frequencies in that part of the body.

The doctor would then put various known remedies in series with the test system to transmit its frequencies to the problem organ or system and if the energy level decreased, it was considered to be an effective remedy for the problem. He would also determine dosage using this method. The Chinese doctor was a licensed and practicing MD in Hawaii so he often tested the drug companies new drug remedies and used some in his healing system. Others he discarded as being far too deadly to use.

Gift of Healing not in All

If we were all blessed with the spiritual gift of healing, such frequency healing systems as described above would not be needed. If our bodies were so full of the Holy Spirit where if any one touched us in faith, they would draw life giving energy from us and be healed instantly. - just like the woman with the issue of blood.

Bitterness Blocks Healing

In all cases, it is well understood that many of our illnesses are caused not by bad substances in our bodies but by bad thinking that brings about buried unforgiveness and bitterness. Bitterness in time will cause physical dissonance and then physical illness. Until the bitterness is resolved and forgiveness granted to the offender, any healing will be temporary and not permanent.

Just Giving Water to the Thirsty

Since we are just 'giving a cup of water to the thirsty' as the remedy with the patients full knowledge of this, it would be difficult for the FDA to control this healing method. If there were Alternative Health Practitioners that would be interested in further studying and applying these methods, I would be interested is sharing what I know as substantial advancements to the Chinese doctors original design.

He used electricity whereas I would use magnetics with a rare 'coil' wind that has pin-point accuracy. However, for me to enter into this field as a practitioner, I would have to spend time in study to fully understand the Meridian energy system of the human body as taught in Acupuncture and other Eastern healing methods.

Perhaps this is the next direction for me that would become a new career. In thinking, all of the devices I have alluded to could fit in a saddle bag and be run on solar energy. This approach would fit well in the coming economic collapse and the decree of Martial Law that will be upon us soon.

Chapter 31: Dream – The Healing Matrix
The Dream

In a dream of the 21st of March, 3013, I found myself in a large group of people. It seemed like the gathering was a convention of some kind related to a church denomination. It was not an Orthodox or Catholic gathering but more non-denominational in character.

I was approached by a man who I could see had a white aura about him. Earlier that evening, I saw him touch someone and healing occurred. When he touched someone for healing, for a moment afterword I could see a pattern of letters in light left behind where he touched them which lasted for only a moment.

The letters were arranged in a long rectangular grid pattern of thee across and 4 down providing for 12 letters that appeared. The grid also shown with light along with the letters. When they all disappeared from my view, the person was healed. I do not know if others could see this light grid and letters but I could.

The man approached me later and sad," Hello." I responded and and said, "I saw what you were doing when healing others." The man then said, "I will teach you this method that I was taught from my teachers." We were sitting on two couches near each other and he asked me to reach over and tough the man behind my couch sitting on another couch facing away from me.

He then said he would impart to me the gift of knowledge [telepathically] so I could also heal like he did. I said the man he wanted me to touch was the leader of the conference and would not understand.

We then both stood up and walked over to a more secluded corner of the large conference room. I then told him that I had seen the script in the light matrix before and suggested it was an Andromadan script.   He said bluntly, "Nope.... it is the same script except for the A and the K but a different language." He then continued and said it was the language of a very "procreative people."

The scene then changed and the man was gone. I then saw a very large creature - aquatic in nature with a small turtle swimming in and out of its mouth. The turtle was feeding on the algae and fungus in the mouth of the creature in cleaning it mouth and teeth that I later realized was a whale.   I thought this must be the creature from which the script and language originated.

I then began to awaken but still in the twilight of sleep, I prayed to YHWH in saying, "What species is this if not Andromadan?"

A couple of the symbols I remember in the grid as indicated in the grid to the right. They seemed at first to be Greek letters to me but were not. The grid and the 12 letters glowed with white light after the touch and then waned to light pink and

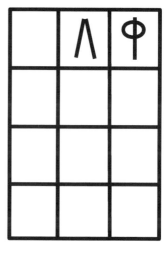

It was as if the light of this grid and letters originated with deep within the skin and then shined out through the skin's surface for about 1-2 seconds then

Still in the twilight of sleep, I was reminded of the Reptilian and Lyra interaction of species and the fall of Atlantis and Lemuria (Mu). The man looked like a human of earth in form but he was not. Neither was he an angel of YWWH. He was a species of higher dimensional origin. I was not sure if others could see him. Perhaps only I was able to see him in his real form.

Still half asleep, I realized the grid provided for reading the letters as words in multiple directions of up, down, left, right and diagonally from the left and right.. This 3 X 4 grid provided for 30 words in this healing matrix made from only 12 letters.

For healing, this text would need to address the very origin of natures power to re-create a part of the human body that had fallen into disrepair. It is very possible that these script characters also represent notes of music and the words in many directions provide for a chord or a sequence of tones that would by the nature of the frequencies sounded would revive the failing cells of the body and renew them to their original state of health.

There are 12 letters in this healing matrix and within the Chromatic scale with 12 one-half step tones in the scale. The playing of these tones as a melody and/or harmonic chord is what is my final understanding of the purpose of this matrix. It continues to sound until the cells are resonate with the energy of the music and are revived and then it disappears. In this case, it only took a few seconds for this to occur.

Chapter 32: The Trinity of Lovemaking
What is love?

Love can provide the greatest form of healing in that it can heal the whole person. Love is light and energy and in its pure form, has more power than any other form of healing remedy. The problem is what is love?

A six year old manages to get his chair close to the table and with great excitement says, "I sure love pizza" as he looks to the oven expecting peperoni pizza to come forth at any moment. Then his sister says, "I love my dolly" that she is holding and gives it a big hug not really paying attention to the pizza event.

Then their mother staring off into space says, "I sure love the vacation to Hawaii" having just returned with her husband a few days earlier.

The husband also disconnected from the pizza event as well as the rest of the comments admits, "I would sure love a martini just now..." In hearing of the love shared by all, I would say they are a very loving family.... wouldn't you?

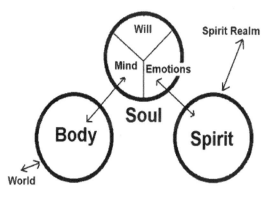

Love is a term that has come to mean little more than words such as 'like' or 'want' in modern English. Yet we find that true love is a healing to the body soul and spirit.

As confusing as this is, the term love is still used during the most intimate moments in lovemaking when a partner says, "I love you" causing the other to perhaps embrace them just a little bit closer.

The problem is the term can easily be misunderstood and wars have been fought over such misunderstandings. I can say that "I love the world' around me but this does not mean I want to have sex with everyone and everything in the world. God forbid (which he does). It is clear that the use of the term 'love' has real meaning only if the context is fully understood.

Lovemaking in Spirit

To not confuse our love for pizza with our love for our partner, there is a sequence of lovemaking that needs to occur to enable true healing love to be birthed. Love making should begin in the realm of the spirit before it is sought in the realm of the soul or the body. How do we do this when we meet someone that we think might be eligible.

I suggest seeking the Creator in prayer and asking for revelation about the spiritual mission of the person you are drawn to. Begin to share what you are hearing and let them either confirm or leave what you are sharing for a later time.

As you share what you are hearing from God, you may see them begin to respond and become caught up in God with you very near them. You then enjoy the joys and revelations of the one you are seeking relationship. This is spiritual love making.

Lovemaking of the Soul

The soul is often divided into the mind or intellect and the heart or emotions. It is hard to say which one should be nurtured first and often such lovemaking of the soul happens to both the mind and heart at the same time.

We hear through the 'ears of the mind and then respond to what we hear and see in facial expressions and body language with emotion. The love making of the spirit can happen at some distance but the lovemaking of the soul is best if the two are together in friendship but not yet sexually active.

At this level of love making, one is sharing about their personal purpose and mission in life as it connects with their journey through this world. The other listens and in their love begin to fully embrace the purposeful life of the other. I will say that people that are caught up in just wanting their own comforts met will never be able to enter into this realm of lovemaking since it must be a self-less approach.

Topics in the lovemaking of the soul may include job future and career directions, home ideas, children, education, finances and more. Human trust is built in this level of lovemaking that causes us to feel very secure with the other. When we just think of them, we feel more completed and whole as a person. Such a form of lovemaking may involve a simple touch of assurance, the holding of hands, a kiss of tenderness but it is not overtly sexual.

It should be noted that sex at this juncture may inhibit the bonding of the two souls to occur to the level that could be possible if they waited. When two people, male and female, are sufficiently bonded first in spirit and then in soul, they are then encouraged to embrace in the physical lovemaking of the body.

I would suggest that when you feel very comfortable with each other with a high level of trust and are not seeking to change the other in their life's mission and goals, then you are ready for the lovemaking of the body. This process can happen very quickly for some but could take years depending on the two involved and the distance they must travel to find each other to then live life together as one soul and one spirit.

Lovemaking of the Body

Finally (I know you were waiting for this) we come to the physical love making of the flesh or body. Most in modern society jump to this first and never experience the lovemaking of the spirit or the soul. Most only have this one strand of the trinity of lovemaking to hold them together through difficult times.

They find the bond is not strong enough and the marriage ends in divorce. Over 50% of western marriages end in divorce and it does not statistically seem to matter if they are Christians, Atheists or whatever.

The lovemaking of the body is very wonderful but it can be 'beyond exceptional' if you are first one in spirit and then one in soul. There is a dimension that can be experienced in physical lovemaking that transcends just the hormonal responses when an act of love becomes a unified trinity in lovemaking. Some say it causes both partners to be lifted up above the earth and experience the creation and healing energy of God himself. In closing, here is a romantic version of the creation story in Genesis.

> **In the beginning, the wind (music) of Creator hovered over the earth and it give forth life from what became water (hydrogen and oxygen) brought forth from the earth. This life was found to be very vibrant and full of fire as lightening (gods life-giving spirit) illuminated from within the four-fold power of earth, water, wind and fire.**

These forces became one in the form of a living spirit who emerged into what God called man – created as male and female. The tow became one in the act of love making as they joined together fully entwined in spirit, soul and body.

Chapter 33: Letter....Priests Married to Nuns?
Email Letter

Here is an email correspondence that occurred recently in response to a very dear woman that feels called to be a nun but has questions that appear to be causing some internal conflict. It may be helpful to others that have had a sense of destiny by Creator in their youth toward Holy Orders but now with life's many challenges and commitments, cannot see how it will ever be possible. Is it possible to fully love and commit to YHWH at the level of a nun while also being married?

Celibacy Not a Requirement for Priesthood

I can assure you it is possible and even preferable to the celibate priesthood as the news tells of uncounted stories of so-called celibate priests engaged in pedophile and fornication. If a man can be a priest and be married as indicated in the Holy Scriptures (Saint Peter was married), should not a woman be able to also be 'set apart' or ordained into ministry and be married? Here is the letter and my response.

Abbot David,

I know what you mean about feeling like an orphan since my mother was only my biological mother and had no love to give, however, when I was about nine years old, I found my true mother in the Blessed Virgin Mary, when an aunt on my father's side gave me a most beautiful statue of the BVM, and I treasured it like it was made of gold.

When I was very young I expressed to my mother that I wanted to be a nun and she discouraged it immediately and said that I really didn't want to become a nun...instead she pushed me toward thinking about becoming a nurse when I grew up...but that didn't stop me from always thinking and dreaming about becoming a nun someday...to live a contemplative prayer life in a convent or in seclusion at a monastery...

Dear sister,

The nuns in our order, the Order of the Culdee, are allowed to marry a priest. The members like most orders take a vow of poverty, chastity and obedience. The chastity is really a commitment of purity to uphold the covenant of husband (priest) and wife (nun) working together in a single ministry representing the full nature of Creator to the world. The nature of Creator is both male and female as indicated by his name as "I AM that I AM" or in Hebrew "Hayah (masculine) Havah (feminine). " If this is your calling.... this is very beautiful and likely a correct leading for your future.

I am the Abbot General of the Order of the Culdee, the oldest Celtic Christian Order in Ireland. When working with the Vatican in research for 25 years, I became the 'Spiritual Guide' as leader of the Culdee for the model of the "Federation of Jesus Abbeys " that Rome once 'blessed' with priests married to nuns established as the personal Prelature of Pope John Paul II. So Rome has at least in principle consented to this model. The issue with Rome has been in not wanting to accept priests who have made vows of celibacy and then married.

The Culdee has always allowed marriage and the women (nuns) were often more influential among the people than the priests whom they married. Many of them function as prophetesses in leading the people to Creator by sharing the very thoughts of Creator to all who would listen.

I find this revelation most revealing about you. It is a direction I would fully support with heart-felt honor.

This correspondence reveals the 2000 year old standard in the Hebrew Celtic churches for the married priesthood that has been even given consideration for adoption by Rome. The Cardinal that was the instigator of the task force mentioned above was Cardinal Ratzinger who only recently resigned as Pope Benedict.

This project resulted in the creation of the Catholic Apostolic Church and the International Ordinariate where I was ordained as a deacon in 1985. It more recently in the 2000's has evolved into the formation of the 'Federation of Jesus Abbeys' that awaits recognition by Pope Francis. See http://jesusabbeys.org

What is the issue preventing a married priesthood in the Roman Church? The fact is the Roman Church does not have enough celibate priests to serve all of the parishes that have congregations. This need is primarily driving this movement within the Roman Church behind secret doors of the Vatican. However, most Roman clergy are opposed to priests who once made vows of celibacy then breaking those vows and becoming married priests within the Roman Church. However Anglican married priests have been received into the Roman Church as priests without issue.

If you ask your local bishop or even your Archbishop, about this project, they will likely not have heard of the study. If you even ask most Cardinals about this study, they will not have heard of it as it was kept very secret.

I know it did exist because I have personally read private letters from former Pope Benedict to Mar (Bishop) John Dunnigan confirming his support and involvement in this project. With the Passing of Mar John, I have been designated the 'spiritual guide' in the formation of the Federation of Jesus Abbeys with the support of the Eastern Church that had association with the Vatican and the Culdee (Celtic Church).

VI. Engaging in Battle

The battle is now upon us. We may not yet see the enemy but it is at our door. I have attempted to open that door in these three books so you as the reader might see the enemy and be motivated to prepare for battle. The enemy is ultimately Satan. The direct children of Satan are the Nephilim. They are the genetic sons of Satan and will carry out his will on this earth as his generals as being both human and angelic.

The Nephilim are super human in many respects but they have a weakness in that they do not love selflessly. Love gives place to no fear and where there is not fear where faith prevails in every cell of your being, you will have supernatural favor from YHWH and will overcome the armies of the Nephilim.

The battles will be bloody and hand to hand combat will become common as new technologies take out virtually all of advanced weaponry on both sides. So many dreams and visions have led me to believe that the final battles will be with sword and horse as fought the knights of old. For a YHWH warrior to be prepared, they should be practicing sword fighting mounted on a horse. This may seem strange and archaic but it may be what saves your life in battle in the end.

I make a plea for knighthood in joining the Order of the Gate. St. Michaels Abbey near Hartsel is set aside for the training of knights in preparation for battle against the Nephilim. If you are called to this noble cause, we have a place for you here to train.

Chapter 34: War with the Nephilim
NWO World Govt by 2012/2017

If you have not been noticing, the occult world is saying they will be in control of all governments around the world by the year 2012 and no later than 2017. Considering the state of the world, I tend to believe them. What this means for true believers is a forced decision for them to comply or they will have to get out of the NWO system while there is still the possibility to do so.

I receive a number of emails from prophets and they are all saying the same warning. We must prepare like the 5 wise virgins and have sufficient oil for our lamps to continue until the Bridegroom comes. This oil is the needed provisions required to be able to see our way with the light of preparation so we are not deceived by the darkness and fall when it comes.

Satanic Seed of the Nephilim

There is a much deeper facet to all this. There are more than one race that lives upon the earth. There are the descendents of Adam and there are the descendents of

Satan (Sama-el) who was in the Garden of Eden and cohabited with Eve and begat Cain. Cain and Seth had different fathers. Seth was fathered by Adam and Cain by Satan.

Even as the flood wiped out this satanic race of Nephilim (except for those who may have escaped underground), fallen angels again cohabited with women after the flood and brought forth another generation of Satanic Nephilim who hated the Adamic race.

The biblical Nephilim are identified in the Canaanite tribes of the Kennites, Anuk, Anikim and Philistines. Esau married into this satanic race by then known as the Hittites and his offspring were mixed with the Satanic seed of the Nephilim. The descendents of Esau became the Edomites and by the 8th century AD were known as the Khazar and converted to Babylonian Judaism and became the majority of the Ashkenazim Jews living today.

The Sephardi Jew have a similar story also connected with the seed of Esau and the Satanic Hittites. Few of the Jews living in Israel are of the seed of Jacob but are a mixed seed of Esau and the Nephilim and follow a Kabbalistic (satanic) form of Judaism developed in Babylon.

This may all seem preposterous but there is extensive documentation on this and this is the understanding held by the Illuminati and the NWO leadership as well as many educated prophets and teachers seeking to warn the Church of the coming difficulty.

The Enemy

The Skeletons of the Nephilim have historically been measured over 36' in length and having 6 fingers on each hand. The giant to the right is over 12 feet tall.

They are not afraid of anything except the coming of Y'Shua in judgment.

The Middle East has graves to this day of the Nephilim who have died. The size unearthed ranges from about 9 feet to 36 feet in height.

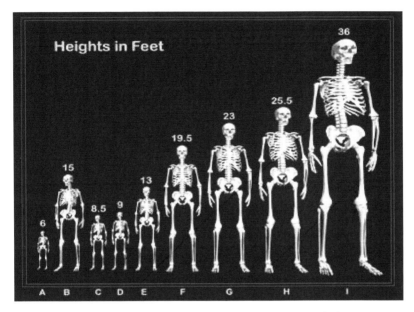

In battle we may not see a Nephilim of this size and height as we as we engage in combat but be aware that this is possible.

Each Nephilim may be seen leading an army of humans into battle as did Goliath of Gath led the Philistines in the wars of the Nephilim against Israel. Once the Nephilim is dispatched, the human followers tend to loose heart and retreat.

War of the Races

The battle for Earth is really a battle over which seed or race will ultimately rule over all the earth. Will it be the seed of Adam as now found in Messiah Jesus (wheat of YHWH) as the second Adam or will it be the seed of Sama-el (Tares of Satan) that started with Cain?

After the flood the process began again with Nimrod of Babylon who was of Nephilim birth. Even the Nephilim were found in the New World as seen in a picture (right) drawn in the early 17th century.

The fallen angels associated with Babylon will provide the 'Satanic' religion for the NWO while its government will be the continuation of the 'unHoly' Roman Empire as the 4th Reich.

All of the large mega churches today in America will either fall under the pressure of the NWO or sell their souls to the NWO to be able to continue to function and make themselves rich. If they resist, they will loose their non-profit status and then loose their properties to the NWO government. These ministers have been deceived and are deceiving the people who attend these big churches that teach what the people want to hear. They are the Laodecean Church spoken of in the book of Revelation and its Says God will spew it out of his mouth. Any church today that is preaching "Peace Peace and Prosperity" is deceived. Only those who are preaching prepare for more difficult times may be in touch with the prophetic words of the true God YHWH.

Chapter 35: Dream- Goliath's Sword Found
The Dream

In the early morning of the 9th of June in 2012, I had a dream where I was in a dense evergreen forest and as I was walking though a small clearing, I saw the hilt of a sword just emerging from the earth. I stopped and reached down and pulled the sword out of the dirt. As I was pulling out the sword, I heard an angel above and behind me say, "The Sword of Goliath... to fight the Nephilim." The sword was rusty and was not fit for battle until it was cleaned and sharpened. My task (as a blacksmith – which I am) was to prepare the sword for battle.

Battle Against the Nephilim

As I awoke, I realized the battle against the Nephilim was coming in great force and that the Church was not prepared for this kind of battle. Thus the sword was rusty and unsharpened. It had to be cleaned and sharpened which is the training of an army to be ready for this kind of battle in the spiritual and physical realm as the 3rd and 4th dimensions merge in these last days..

The necessity of the full Armor of God was also needed and must be rightly fitted to each warrior since the battle was first spiritual and then played out in the physical world. I believe the future battles will be very real with real swords and with real armies but only the pure in heart and the faithful will be victorious in battle against the Nephilim. It is reality that such wars are first fought and won in the spiritual realm that will determine the outcome of who lives and dies in the physical realm.

Chapter 34: Dream – War Against the Dragons

In the early morning of the 3rd of June 2013, I had a dream where I found myself on a great battle field. The field was a plain - almost a desert and could have been somewhere in the Middle East. It was a warm day and the battle was fierce. I saw humans fighting dragons and other draconian or reptilian creatures that looked half human and half beast.

As the battle continued, some of the humans who had fallen rose up from near death and then took on certain characteristics of the dragon. The wounds inflicted by both sides were very graphic with cuts deep into the chest where the entrails were clearly exposed. Death for such wounds was eminent.

As I watched, I noticed that some of the humans who had fallen would appeal to the power of the Dragon to save them from death and heal them. I would then see massive motile wounds begin to heal before my eyes with their guts being sucked back into the body and then chests close and heal within minutes.

The human then stood up ready for battle but there was a change that occurred to the human after this healing by the Dragons. These humans who had appealed to the Dragons for healing began to mutate into the likeness of a dragon with horns, great teeth, scales, and claws appearing.

Then I heard the voice of what I what I thought was an angel cry out and say, "All who seek the power to heal from the Dragon are no longer man but have given their souls to the Dragon from which there is no return."

I then saw the once human knights who had fallen and given themselves to the healing power of the Dragons become a human/dragon mutation and now rise to fight for the cause of the great Dragon who is Satan. They then turned on their once brothers and other humans. Just minutes ago, they were friends and comrades in arms and now they were enemies and would seek to kill the humans without mercy.

Brothers would fight against brothers with one now taking the form of a dragon hybrid and fully committed to battle to the death by the sword. In one scene I saw myself fighting with full armor and the sword against my own brother. He as a human had been mortally wounded and then called upon the Dragon to spare his life and heal him. This request was granted and now he was destined to face his own brother, me, in battle as a draconian knight.

He came after me singling me out from the other human knights and pursued me into a pool of water where the battle engaged. I had no choice but to fight or die. I asked my self, "Was this my brother or had he been completely taken over by the dark side and now had no knowledge of what he was doing?" I was not sure what was the truth on this question. I tried to avoid his advances but I could not. Our father was also in the pool as he watched his two sons fight to the death. His pleas for us to stop were not heard as the fight continued with swords slashing to get a solid contact with the flesh of the other.

Finally I was able to inflict a mortal blow and my now Draconian brother stopped fighting and began to die. As if for a moment, he regained his human senses and I could see in his eyes he realized what he had done with great remorse. He seemed to understand there was no way to get free from the Draconian hold on his soul.

You see... my brother had willingly taken the Mark of the Beast in his forehead in requesting and receiving the healing power of the Dragon to save his life. In so doing, he made Satan his lord and master and choose against YHWH. He then took the Mark of the Beast in his hand in taking up the sword of murder against his own brother who fought for the cause of Y'Shua and YHWH. The Mark of the Beast is a seal upon the soul from which there can be no escape. My brother then closed his eyes as he lay upon the ground in a pool of blood and the dream ended.

This dream was very unnerving in that is was close to home and involved the people I love. I have come to accept that this dream is a warning of what is to come and how we as Christian Knights must be faithful even to death to avoid being brought under the power of the Dragon who is Satan. I love my brother Jonathan and pray he will be strong to the very end and not give his soul to the Dragon to live.

I believe this is a real future event - perhaps a snapshot of a scene in the battle of Armageddon when all creation will be engaged in battle on the earth. This means angels, humans and aliens as these are counted in creation. Lord.... have mercy upon us your people and warriors.

Chapter 36: Patriots vs. Socialists

In America there is still the US Constitution that is paid lip service by the Government and Courts. Neither of these two institutions along with the houses of Congress really follow the US Constitution as is evidenced in the recent passing of the Health Care Bill, Patriot Acts and other Executive Orders. Some have called this new force the NWO or the Progressive movement which is just another word for socialism forced upon the American people.

The two common forms of socialism

Socialism expresses itself commonly as either a Fascist government or a Communist government. It does not really matter which one is imposed because both forms remove any vestige of sovereignty from the individual and invest it into the government of a few who then control the masses with promises of equality.

Biblical Giving

The bible teaches us "Let each man decide in his own heart what he is to give and to give willingly and not of necessity [by force]" I believe this is the general principle of giving and applies to tithing and also to taxes in the support of government and applies to anything that we give. The Preamble of the US Constitution clearly cites "inalienable rights" as given to us by our Creator as the justification for our individual sovereignty where no King or government should be allowed to take this away and tell us how to live.

We are Slaves

The US Constitution also encourages any citizen to rise up against any force of government whether internal or external that would seek to take these inalienable rights away. Sadly, we have become mere tenets or serfs on our own lands in having to pay taxes or really rent for the property we use.

With the added imposition of laws against gun ownership, access to water, burdensome rules for business, valueless currency and the removal of all energy and mineral rights, we have little left we can really call our own. Now with forced healthcare where even our continence of life is at the decision of the government, we have lost most all of the rights afforded to us by the US Constitution. We have become mere slaves and most Americans don't even realize this or don't care. When is it time to say enough is enough?

Nazi Socialist Rerun

The process of decline that occurred in Nazi Germany was less than 80 years ago. The Nazi fascist-socialists were the progressive movement of its day and by the time the German people woke up to what was happening, there rights were all gone and their guns were already confiscated.

They were defenseless as sheep led away for the slaughter under a demonic police state. America is on the very same track and it may not take any longer than 2013 for all to be in place for the US Constitution to be completely disbanded in exchange for a New World Order 'collective' dictatorship.

Prepare for Battle

Since Y'Shua is soon returning - not as a lamb for sacrifice but as a warrior King to bring war against the Antichrist and those of the NWO that hate the truth, I believe we are to prepare for the same. I believe our first course of action is get unhooked from the government controlled food, energy, illegal tax and health care systems. Get out of stocks, bonds and retirement accounts and invest in remote land where you can grow food, harness alternative energy and live from the resources the land provides.

Set aside in store whole grains and non-hybrid GMO seeds and know where to hunt game. Being a Patriot is not going to war in Iraq or Afghanistan as these wars were spawned by the NWO to remove any resistance to their global control of fossil fuels. Being a Patriot is in opposing socialism right here at home including the HOA's and County and City governments that seek to become the masters of our lands and demand we follow their plan in dictating how we may live on our lands.

The individual people of the United States are the only legal sovereign Government and not the elected officials. The elected can only do what we tell them to do according to the US Constitution. If they are not doing the will of the people, they are committing treason against the people of the United States and need to be removed from office and tried for treason in a 'peoples' court.

Who are the real Patriots?

Patriot Americans were once called the 'Sons of Liberty' during the Revolutionary War. Again we need to draw the line in the sand and gather together as communities in preparing for war in remote areas to protect the biblical rights afforded to us by the US Constitution.

If you stay in the cities, effective resistance will not be possible.

If you stay in the suburbs of the cities or on major transportation routes, effective resistance will not be possible.

If your dependence remains on fossil fuels and food grown by the conglomerates, effective resistance will not be possible.

If you have not learned how to harness the energy of wood, solar, wind or water and can survive in wilderness areas, effective resistance will not be possible.

If you are preparing for more difficult times and still work for income in the city, you may only have a few hours to get out of the city and get to your prepared place. before the roads are locked down. Do you have a plan for this?

It is possible Martial Law will occur overnight as you are sleeping and the roads will be closed to travel when you wake up in the morning. In such a case, you will not be allowed to leave the city to get to your safe place.

What if your wife or husband disagrees with this concern yet you are convinced of the need to prepare, what can you do? I suggest finding others of the same concern and then meeting with them in seeking to do what you can do to prepare a place with them for your family.

Let the HS Lead You

Ultimately, it is the Lord Y'Shua [Jesus] that must guide you through the Holy Spirit and what I am suggesting here is to be tempered by the Holy Spirit for each person. There is not one universal plan for everyone. Neither am I suggesting forming a revolutionary militia since our warfare is first in the spirit and secondly in the natural. We have to win in the heavenlies in faith before we can expect to win any battle here on earth in the natural. Lastly, we are to walk in faith, hope and love in all decision making and not by fear.

Chapter 37: Dream- Puppet Theater of the Word

The Dream

In the early morning of the 16th of June, I had a dream where I saw a number of gypsy styled wagons with the sides having large openings set up as a mobile stage for puppet theater. As I watched in this dream I saw a group of wagons being pulled by various vehicles by puppeteers traveling from

place to place to provide shows about the teachings of the Bible and to deliver prophetic messages.

Self-Sufficient Wagons

The puppeteers lived in these wagons that had beds and a small wood stove for heating and cooking. Each wagon was completely self-contained in its ability to travel most anywhere to perform. The wagons had 12 VDC powered sound systems built in so performing to large crowds was

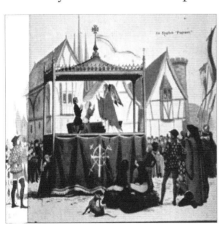

possible. On the roofs of the wagons were solar voltaic panels for charging the 12 VDC batteries to run lighting and the sound system.

'Wagon Train' Ministry

I then saw in the dream this team of puppeteers stopping at Mall parking lots, rest stops, large gas stations or other public places and just start performing puppet shows to those walking by.

The wagons were observed making a circle in large parking lots and providing plays from the different wagons to a group gather in the center.

Folding chairs were provided for the audience One wagon would do a short play then the next in rotation. The team visited churches on Sundays to perform at sponsored events outside. The team was seen gathering to pray each morning to be led by the Holy Spirit as to when and where they would perform that day. I then awoke form this dream.

Easy Fit for Me

In considering this dream, I admitted to myself I am a builder of wagons. I am now praying about this dream asking if it is what I am to be doing now for more effectively getting the message out to the American people and to others we meet.

The need is now for the sharing of the good news of the Gospel and the prophetic message about the need for all to prepare for the coming political-economic collapse. This collapse will bring with it many difficulties into the world in these last days and many will die because they are not prepared.

With a college background in theater production and puppet theater, this would be a natural and easy direction for me to pursue in ministry.

The scripts for the puppets can be very diverse with added music and singing employing opera, country, rock, pop, or any music style possible.

Actors could wear full body puppet costumes or period costumes who would perform in front of the puppet wagons to better interact with the audience. Hand and marionette puppets would also be used in performance.

Theme Wagon 'Sets'

With many wagons traveling together, the wagons could be built after a biblical theme like the wagons were in the mystery plays of the Medieval ages. If the story or message was about Satan or the rise of the Antichrist or hell, it could be a 'dragon' and hell-hole looking wagon set for this message.

If the message was about the 10 Commandments, it could be a wagon looking like a mountain with smoke with a Tabernacle set on the mountain where Moses received the 10 Commandments from God (YHWH). If it was about Jonah and the great fish in teaching that we cannot escape from God, it could be a ship designed wagon.

Funding is always a challenge for such ventures but first one must be convinced it is the leading of the Lord to do now in this time and place before funding can be expected to become available. Keep this in your prayers and contact me if you would like to participate in the development of this traveling ministry.

If we get enough interested in wanting to commit to this ministry, it can be very possible. This ministry could be put together most anywhere and travel in the southern US during the winter months and in the northern States during the summers. It could even travel into Europe and toward the Middle East on a Pilgrimage to Jerusalem. This could become a troubadour life-style for many in sharing the Gospel to the needy in the difficult years ahead.

Chapter 38: Priests and Bishops in War
Warrior Bishops and the Mace

Originally, the mace was a weapon, effectively a wooden club, larger and heavier at one end. Warrior bishops carried it into battle instead of the sword, in order to conform to the canonical rule forbidding the shedding of blood by members of the clergy.

The Bayeux Tapestry (a full length reproduction of which can be seen in Reading Guild Hall), depicts the Battle of Hastings and shows only Odo, Bishop of Bayeux armed with a mace.

With the introduction of armor, the original wooden club became less effective as a weapon and so was bound with iron to make it heavier and more deadly in battle. By the time of the 11th and 12th Centuries, the mace was almost entirely made of iron or steel.

At this time it was close fighting where armored men used an iron or steel mace roughly two feet long. One end would be molded into a ball fitted with spikes, which would be capable of penetrating either armor or an adversary's helmet.

The other end of the mace was the hand grip with a small knob to prevent the mace from slipping out of the hand or mailed glove. By the time of Henry VIII, the mace was in general use by knights at military sports events such as jousting tournaments.

Battle without Shedding Blood

Warrior bishops existed as recorded in church history as early as the 4th century of the Christian era. By Economy, the early church believed in the art [action] of doing what was possible when a higher ideal of a godly peace was not sustained.

In the case of war, Basil and the canonical tradition are tacitly saying that when the Kingdom ideals of peace and reconciliation collapse, especially in times of war when decisive and unusual action is required. When the ideals of reconciliation and forgiveness fall into chaos in the very heart, then war is justified against the offenders.

The Church then is called to go out as members to fight where the ideal of truth can be reasserted as soon as possible — with limitations to the hostilities a primary concern, and a profound desire to mark the occasion retrospectively with a public "cleansing."

While the honor of the combatants is celebrated by Basil (even demanded as an act of protection for the weak), one essential aspect of that honor is also listed as being the public acceptance of the status of penitent shedding of blood.

The clergy (as with other economic concessions of morality operative in the church's canons) are the only ones not allowed benefit of necessity. In no case is violent action permitted to one who stands at the altar of God. Even if a cleric spills blood accidentally (such as in an involuntary manslaughter) such a person would be deposed from active presbyteral office.

However, this was not held by the Church universally and many exceptions were made through out history. Even in Israel, the prophet Elijah hacked off the heads of the 400 prophets of Baal and this was accepted as righteous judgment by YHWH.

The sight of "warrior- bishops" in full military regalia, passing through the streets of Constantinople in the Fourth Crusade, left its mark on contemporary Greek sources.

Bishop Odo of Bayeux

Bishop Ordo lived from c. 1036 – February, 1097, Palermo [1]) and reigned as a Norman bishop and English earl. He was the half-brother of William the Conqueror, and was for a time second only to the king in wealth and power in England.

He was the son of William the Conqueror's mother Herleva, and Herluin de Conteville. Count Robert of Mortain was his younger brother. There is some uncertainty about his birth date. Some historians have suggested he was born as early as 1030, so that he would be about 19 instead of 14 when William made him bishop of Bayeux in 1049.

Although he was an ordained Christian cleric, he is best known as a warrior and statesman. He found ships for the invasion of England and was present at the Battle of Hastings.

In 1067 Odo became Earl of Kent, and for some years he was a trusted royal minister. On some occasions when William was absent (back in Normandy), he served as *de facto* regent of England, and at times he led the royal forces against rebellions (eg the Revolt of the Earls). The precise sphere of his powers is not certain, however. There are also other occasions when he accompanied William back to Normandy.

During this time Odo acquired vast estates in England, larger in extent than any one except the king's. He had land in 23 counties, primarily in the southeast and in East Anglia.

Fighting Bishop General Polk

Leonidas Polk was born in Raleigh, North Carolina, on April 10, 1806. He attended the University of North Carolina, then was appointed to the US Military Academy at West Point, where he was deeply influenced by the chaplain. Graduating in 1827, he resigned his commission soon after graduation and entered Virginia Theological Seminary. Ordained a deacon in the Episcopal Church in 1830, he was appointed missionary bishop to the Southwest in 1836.

After being named missionary bishop of the southwest, Polk traveled extensively. His territory included Tennessee, Arkansas, Louisiana, and Mississippi. Named bishop of Louisiana in 1841, he began a long, but successful campaign to establish an Episcopal university in the South, which became the University of the South (Swanee).

In 1838 the Diocese of Louisiana was organized and in 1841 the Rt. Rev. Leonidas Polk was appointed by the General Convention of the Episcopal Church in the United States as the first Bishop of the new Diocese. Bishop Polk had been a Missionary Bishop of the Southwest and was responsible for the founding and consecration of many congregations in Louisiana. He was also the first foreign missionary Bishop of the Episcopal Church as his oversight extended also to the Republic of Texas. Bishop Polk, a graduate of West Point, was to serve the Confederacy during the American Civil War as a General in the Army.

He also was the leading founder of the University of the South in Swanee, Tennessee. Adopting secession as a sacred cause, Bishop Polk withdrew from the Episcopal Convention of Louisiana of the Episcopal Church of the United States, resigned and returned to the military where Confederate President Davis appointed him a major general in the Provisional Confederate Army.

Placed in command of Department No. 2, he later fought at the Belmont, Shiloh and Perryville, after which he was promoted (took rank from October 10, 1862). Polk took part in the fighting at Stone's River, but Gen. Braxton Bragg ordered that he face a court-martial after failing to attack [to save his men] as planned at Chickamauga.

Confederate President Davis, in an attempt to ease tensions between Bragg and Polk, placed Polk in command of the Department of Alabama, Mississippi and East Louisiana. Unable to counter Union Maj. Gen. William T. Sherman's march from Vicksburg to Meridian, Polk's troops were reinforced by the Army of Tennessee, under the command of Gen. Joseph E. Johnston. On June 14, 1864, while spying on the Union positions from the top of Pine Mountain, Polk was killed by an artillery shell.

Comment

The paradigm of warrior-bishops is not just a curious happening of Medieval history but also a historic fact as recently as the American Civil War. Episcopal Bishop Poke of Louisiana became a Major-General in the forces of the Confederate States and led his armies against the invading Federalists and died from wounds sustained in battle. He has recently been honored as a Martyr for his fight against the aggression of the North by the **Episcopal Church** in the South.

He was noted as a man of prayer, baptized many of the other Confederate generals and was affectionately known as General Bishop Poke or the 'Fighting-Bishop'.

Today, we face the prospect of the New World Order and the invading Nephilim and Islamic forces who clearly state they intend to destroy our western culture and our right to hold faith in Jesus as our messiah. The New World Order and Islamic extremists have already proven they are committed to more than just threat with the bombings in many western cities in Europe.

One can only wonder if it is not time for bishops of the Christian Church to rally again under a banner of holy resistance as Crusaders in leading armies against such hell-bent groups we now term as terrorists. I believe it is time for another holy Crusade to resist evil in this world.

Chapter 39: Swords of the Highlander
Three Swords

Recently, I was given three swords and two daggers based on the movie the 'Highlander'. The main actor was a surviving McLeod that would live forever if he could keep his head from becoming severed from his body. My closest connection to the Macleod's was my first girl friend, Julie McLeod, and we would ride a white horse together bareback in Oregon as a kid. I still remember the pointed backbone of this most uncomfortable elderly horse.

The reoccurring theme in the movie is "There can only be one." This factor drove these 'eternal life' warriors to find others if the same gifting and kill them before being killed by them. There were two camps and often two of the good would travel together to war against the evil ones.

In the end, there can only be one remaining alive so even the two good would have to fight each other eventually or one would have to be killed by evil along the way. The implication is the remaining one was to become a benefactor over the rest of the earth when evil was finally dispatched from the earth. This is very much a Messiah concept where super-human good and evil battle it out and in the end, good overcomes evil and rules the earth. I wonder where they got this concept?

Goliath's Sword

In the Japanese culture among the Samurai, the sword would honor and protect the warrior as long as the warrior honored his superiors and honored the family soul within the sword. King David was said to have taken the sword of Goliath and used it in battle against the Philistines.

The design of the sword was likely similar to the common Philistine design that has been unearthed today (picture above). Perhaps Goliath, as did many knights in Europe, also had a short sword that King David used since Goliath's full-sized sword would be too much weight for an averaged sized man to wield.

Some have theorized that the sword Excalibur that was said to be pulled from the stone by Arthur was formerly the Sword of King David brought to Ireland by Jeremiah in about 500 BC or by the Queens of Avalon much later in history. It was thought this sword become the symbol of the 'right of kingship' over the Hebrew-Celts. It may well have been Goliath's original sword as illustrated.

Some tribes of the Philitines were known to be of Nephilim (fallen angel and human women hybrid) stock and were very skilled in metallurgy. They were far superior in this science than the Hebrews at the time and it was from the Philistines that King David got his first steel for sword making.

Sword of the Spirit

The bible speaks of the Sword of the Spirit which is the Word of God as the primary offensive weapon for Christians to wield against the temptations of demons and fallen angels.

In medieval times, hand to hand combat was considered the test for guiltless truth as the victor was considered to be vindicated by God in the killing of his opponent.

The sword was then considered the tool of judgment in the hands of the righteous that God would protect against evil. We certainly get this ideal from the battle between David and Goliath when a young lad in rough woven desert wear kills with a rock a fully armored and seasoned warrior who stood between 9' and 12' tall depending on if you use the Hebrew Cubit or the Egyptian cubit in measurement. It was clear that God judged between them and Goliath was found without grace (favor) from God.

Blood of Armageddon

In the future, the book of Revelation speaks of the blood the dead filling the valley of Megeddo up to the horses bridle. That is about 3 feet deep.

"And the wine press was trodden outside the city [Jerusalem], and blood came out of the wine press even unto the horse bridles, by the space of a thousand and six hundred furlongs." (200 miles) Rev. 14:20

Is this prophecy figurative or literal? In the course of battle, if all of the computerized war machinery were short-circuited by EMF bombs and solar flares from the sun, what would be left. Solar flares are to be in the extreme between around 2008-2017 with sufficient power to disable most all of our US based computer systems that control communications, electrical power and transportation. They are putting computer chips in small arms now to prevent unauthorized use so these too could be disabled.

Would we be left with only the sword as the final weapon of mass destruction? Would we be left with the horse as the only means of transportation since most all vehicles are computer chip controlled? No aircraft would be flying or any smart missiles.

You would have over 200,000,000 warriors staring at each other in the valley of Megeddo also named Armageddon and ready for battle – perhaps only supplied with the simplest weapons of battle. If I were to fight in such a battle, I would be riding a horse and certainly have a good sword with me just in case.

Where is the Highlander

So... where is the Highlander when you need him? Is Jesus to become the final "There only can be one" after evil is dispelled from the earth? You cannot get any more 'highland' than to the heights of heaven. It does say Jesus comes on a white charger (a horse – not a dodge muscle car or flying saucer) with a sword in hand to make war against the antichrist and the Beast.

I have vowed that Jesus is my highlander King and I will follow him and no other. Blessed be the name of YHWH!

Chapter 40: Culdee as Prophet-Priests at War

Culdee as Chaplains

The Culdee are prophet-priests and are noted in history as far bask as 500 BC when Jeremiah came to Ireland. The term Culdee has been translated as the 'Servants of God' and it is likely derived from the term 'Kadeem' which means 'servant' in Arabic as derived from an earlier proto-Hebrew form which means 'holy unto god'.

Our current call is to provide Chaplains to various noble houses to serve as spiritual advisers and confessors to bring unity to the Church and to Christian nations.

Working with Nobles

It can be challenging to work with persons of noble birth as many of these leaders have a profound sense of vision and destiny and have been raised to overcome every challenge that would question their destiny. At times they may appear to be overly arrogant and unbending but this is really a positive virtue once truth is their foundation in life. I can say that this trait is needed to hold honorably to the truth of Y'Shua and overcome those who oppose the call of YHWH in their lives.

Royal Abuses

Many Americans still live in the illusion of national independence from all royal rulers and do not have the life context for what I am seeking to share here. The political ideal of a Kingdom is the highest form of government as presented in the Holy Scriptures with Y'Shua soon to come as the King of Kings to begin his 1000 year rule over the earth.

This is not a Republic or Democracy but a Monarchy. What about the many historic abuses by royals? What is needed is to assure there is a balance of power in a nation acceptable by all citizens.

Did you know that instead of a presidency, the new US Congress circa 1776 offered to George Washington the position of King of the United States as he was of royal lineage? He turned it down so we now have settled for a President.

What is interesting is that most all of the US presidents can trace their genealogy to some royal house in Europe. What is alarming is that many of the recent Presidents have paid fealty to the Queen of England in receiving knighthood. This could be considered treachery against the US Constitution and the American people.

Three Courts and Military

I have proposed that there be three courts of judgment that can judge any matter. This proposal addresses the needed balance of power doctrine that is also embraced in most of the democratic western nations. The three courts would include the Royal Court setup for International Relations. The Civil Courts of the people to assure ethics and law are equally upheld for all and an Ecclesiastical Court of the Church that would deal with matters of royal, church and civic morality.

Most violations against society have a dimension that is moral (spiritual), civil (ethical) and a royal (sovereignty) component to it. Keep in mind that to be sovereign such is the state of all Americans, it is a royal right we have all been given by the US Constitution.

Where then should the military or police be placed so there will not be a ready abuse of police power? I have proposed that any military or police force be under the direction of the Civil Courts for domestic peace keeping and under the crown for foreign peace keeping.

The Church would monitor the morality of the military through its chaplains. Any one of the courts can call someone to give account of their deeds done. The death penalty and declaration of war could be enacted by an agreement of all three courts.

Royal Claims

What we will see in the days to come is the rise of royal houses of the seed of King David of Israel. These houses will be making claim on former lands around the world. We will also see ancient knightly orders revived as a new military and police force subject themselves to the emerging Y'Shua governments.

Chaplains will become a very important part of the Y'Shua government where there really is no separation of Church and State. The notion of a separation of Church and State is not biblical and is logically ridicules. It is like thinking a person can function with a fully disconnected (lobotomy disconnect) conscience and intellect in decision making. The Church is the conscience of the State and the Royals the protectors of the Church.

Where will we see this first occur? Some historic states with a ruling king were no larger than the size of a town or city. The Vatican City is a sovereign State accepted as a member of the UN yet is less than 10 acres in size. It was not uncommon to give sovereignty to an Abbey with 10 miles around the abbey as the sole and sovereign territory of the abbey. No king would normally claim the legal right to tax or rule the territory of the Abbey as the Abbey had their own knights and army and would be a force to reckon with.

We see this as the case with the Templars until the Vatican in partnership with the greedy king of France ruled they were heretics and by force confiscated all their holdings. I believe such an appeal to this historic model would work today on lands that are in dispute where a noble birth right is still a valid claim under international law.

If the noble heir of the land were to come forward and reassert his or her rightful claim on the land, it would have to be considered legally theirs under international law.

Europe and Israel

Over the last year, I have met a number of individuals that are seeking to reclaim their noble or royal inheritance with claims that date back hundreds or even thousands of years. Many of these nobles bow their knee in fealty to King Y'Shua and acknowledge Y'Shua is the King of all Kings. If the Culdee can provide chaplains in this effort and evangelize the people by preaching the Gospel and call them to come to Y'Shua as Lord and Savior, we are doing our mission.

I am aware of a move to reclaim lands in Europe and a 'presence' in the former lands of Ephraim near Shilo, Israel to prepare for the return of the 10-tribes to northern Israel. Genetic Judah will also return to the lands in southern Israel along with the Levites and reclaim Jerusalem for the true seed of Jacob. This is prophesied to occur in the Holy Scriptures before the return of Messiah.

Chapter 26: Knights of the Order of the Gate
History of the Order

The Knights of the Order of the Gate of Jerusalem was founded in 1985 by bishop Mar John Dunnigan who was a bishop serving within the personal Prelature of Pope John Paul II. The original mission of this Prelature was to provide a sacramental home for married Roman priests in the Syro-Chaldean Church then called the Catholic Apostolic Church / International Ordinariate (Eastern Rite).

Abbot-Bishop David Michael (his seal to the right) was ordained a Deacon within

this Papal Prelature in 1985 and was elected as the Abbot and Grand Master of the Order of the Gate by Bishop Mar John. In recent years, the Order has taken on a Chivalric nature in conferring knighthood while still holding to the religious vows of prayer, poverty, chastity and obedience.

The call of this Order is to prepare for the wars that are coming soon against the Nephilim, their fathers as the fallen angels called 'watchers' by Enoch and their human and alien allies.

This alien species does not have the yDNA genetic line to Adam but to Sama-el who was the serpent in the Garden of Eden who deceived both Adam and Eve with the promise of wisdom.

Armor of the Order

The armor of the Order is modern and focuses on stealth capabilities rather than taking the brunt of an attack. The chosen model is to engage the enemy without being seen with a full commitment to stealth. The color of uniforms are chosen for each engagement in order to blend into the surroundings. Weapons chosen are silent and the movement of speed is required using non-metallic vehicles when possible in preferring the horse.

Vows of the Order

The vows of the Order are simple. Prayer is a biblical command in our being instructed to "Pray without ceasing." Poverty is in not holding anything as your own but offering all for the mission of Y'Shua and his Generals who lead the Armies of YHWH as given to the Order.

Chastity is in being either single or married and holding to these covenants you have made before God and man. If married, remain fully committed to this covenant and to the woman to whom you gave your vows. If single, remain chaste in not being tempted and drawn into fornication.

Obedience is first being obedient to the tenets of the Holy Scriptures and then in clear conscience being obedient to the directives of the Grand Master of the Order.

The Order of the Gate is a gathering place for priest-prophet-warriors where training must be acquired in all areas including fighting with the sword and horse. This is a forerunner to the gathering of the 144,000 prophet-warriors who will be led by Y'Shua and YHWH after the middle of the 7 year tribulation period.

Training

Each knight of the Order of the Gate in training will learn to hear and obey the voice of the Holy Spirit in being led and empowered by YHWH to be able to defeat the Nephilim enemy.

This enemy is smart (100-300 IQ), fast in movement and many can read your mind. Only the fearless in faith and pure of heart will survive such an encounter in battle with the Nephilim.

You may ask what then is the possibility of survival in such an encounter? We are to understand that as we fight with a purity of heart, the warrior angels of YHWH fight along with us in overcoming such unreasonable odds. "If YHWH is for us, who can be against us" says the Holy Scriptures.

Sword and Horse

Some may wonder why the focus on the sword and horse in this chapter. I can tell you there are weapons already invented that can heat up the metal of a gun and fuse its moving parts together so it does not function.

Although it can also heat up a sword, there are no moving parts to fuse together. Since vehicles are metal predominately in their engines, the engine parts will also be fused making the vehicle useless. Would you rather be swinging a sharp sword or a blunt gun butt at your enemy in a hand to hand battle for your life?

To prove the viability of this kind of weapon, simply put a metal pan in the microwave and turn it up to high and watch what happens. **(don't really do this)** You will see sparking and the pan melt if left in for just a few seconds. When you open the microwave to pull the pan out realizing your error, it will be too hot to touch. Such is the simple technology employed for the metal fusing weapons.

Legal Structure

To be a 501c3 corporation is to exist at the pleasure of the US Government. You have no Constitutional protections as a corporation. Most big churches and TV preachers will continue to function under the NWO and fall into even greater deception. Many have already sold their souls in embracing the greed of money in teaching the prosperity "name it and claim it" heresy. If your church is teaching this heresy doctrine, warn others against it and get out ASAP as it has already been infiltrated by NWO leadership.

The Order of the Gate has no US Government legal permission to exist. We gain our right of existence from YHWH alone.

Communal Living

As much as we may find the idea of a commune objectionable, this is the mostly likely model to survive difficult times by sharing resources among a group of people in "having all things common." This was the model for the first converts reported in Acts 2.

I grew up between the ages of 12 and into my 20's living in Christian communes including Shiloh Ranch (Eugene, OR), Lighthouse Ranch (Eureka, CA) and the Fellowship of Christian Pilgrims in Hawaii.

I can tell you there are pros and cons to living in a commune where all is shared but in a time of severe duress, this will prove to be the best model for preserving the remnant of the faithful. St. Michaels Abbey near Hartsel CO exists as a simple commune of believers.

No city will be a safe place for true believers as your neighbors will be tasked as informants to expose anyone who is not in full and open support of the NWO regime. We already see this kind of accepted social control of neighbors in the form of Property Owners Associations that tell you what are acceptable plants, paint colors, animals and what you can have in your yard.

If you would like help in finding others in your area who are wanting to prepare for more difficult times, let us know and if we hear of someone in your area also seeking to do the same, we would be happy to refer you.

Call to Knighthood

The call goes out from the Grand Master of the Order of the Gate to gather 300 knights into the Order before the end of 2013. As an Order, we are called to forge an alliance with the Native American as per the existing Covenant of the Anasazi. (see book 1 for more detail on this covenant).

When YHWH is ready, we will make a pilgrimage to Jerusalem to reclaim Jerusalem for the Hebrew Church founded by the family of Y'Shua that has been in exile among the Celts for 2000 years. We will then travel to Acre in Lebanon to gather the armies of the 1000 Caliphates in the Middle East. These although Muslim in faith will stand with us to resist the invasion of the Middle East by the NWO forces coming down from the North.

We will then find a place in Jordan to prepare for the escape of the true Church to Petra. All this has been prophesied and will come to pass as YHWH enables us. Blessed be the name of the Lord YHWH who is the one God above all other gods!

Books and Workshops

Abbot David has lived in the mountains of Colorado at near 10,000 foot elevation for the last 5 years as a Franciscan Friar and has given himself to prayer and study with the results found in this book. He is a Culdee (Celtic) priest and Templar.

This third book of the NWO series provides even more dreams and studies about the end times that are upon us. It provides solutions to be prepared for the disaster that is to come upon the earth.

As a followup to this book, I am writing a field manual for those seeking to war effectively against evil angelic, demonic and alien forces who oppose YHWH. The book titled, "Templar and Culdee" seeks to teach spiritual warriors how to battle in the 3rd and 4th dimensional world and above.

If the reader would like Abbot-Bishop David Michael to visit your group to provide workshops on the content of this trilogy of books, please go to http://glentivar.org and propose an arrangement for him to come to visit you. It is the desire and leading of Abbot David to travel throughout the US and Europe to bring encouragement to the people of YHWH with clarity on the topics presented in his books.

For more information, you may contact Abbot David at:

Abbot David
POB 301
Hartsel, Co 80449

http://glentivar.org
info@glentivar.org
719 421 9109

Ordering: https://www.createspace.com/4181579
Contact Abbot David directly for bulk orders of 10 or more books so you can receive a discount code.

18218984R00124

Made in the USA
San Bernardino, CA
05 January 2015